Reclaiming Adolescents

A Return to the Village State of Mind

by Chaim Peri

Wisdom on Education and Parenting

from Yemin Orde Youth Village

Jay Street Publishers, New York, NY 10023

ISBN   1-889534-80-3

Published by Jay Street Publishers
155 West 72nd Street, New York, NY 10023

Table of Contents

Acknowledgements

This book was born into the world through the efforts of two extraordinary individuals: Henry and Edith Everett of New York City.

Through their special, long-standing interest in youth and in the future of the State of Israel, Henry and Edith learned of Yemin Orde and observed our work here first hand. From that point onwards the Everetts became our partners, in heart and in soul. Henry, to whose blessed memory this book is dedicated, saw the exposure of our work in Yemin Orde to a wider public as an important mission. His interest in our work was so deep and meaningful that, after already been taken ill, and before having fully recovered from a serious operation, he insisted on accompanying Edith and myself to Hershey, Pennsylvania, in order to learn from the renowned boarding school that was Milton Hershey's legacy, and to compare their ideas and methodology with our work in Israel.

After Henry's painful passing, Edith did everything in her power in order to insure that this book would become a reality.

Here is the place to express a debt of gratitude to Micha Odenheimer of Jerusalem, a writer and highly regarded journalist, and a friend whose devotion to Ethiopian Jewry first created a connection between us. Micha was the living spirit behind the process through which this book was written. The contents of the book grew out of the many hours we sat together in deep conversation. Without him the book would not have been written at all. The conditions of my work with the children in Yemin Orde would never have enabled me to escape the flow of life – its power would have triumphed over me. Under these circumstances, finding the focus and concentration necessary for the writing of a book is not one of the privileges with which I have been blessed. Micha, with a great deal of patience, stayed with me until this manuscript emerged. He invested in this process not only his professional skills, but also his soul.

Our ability to sustain an educational community here on Mt. Carmel would not be possible without the help of many partners. Without them, the reality from which the book has grown would not exist.

In this context I would like to thank Mark Solomon and Paul Silverberg, both of Philadelphia, Pennsylvania. For many years, and with great dedication, they have headed the *Friends of Yemin Orde* – an organization run successfully by Susan Pollack from Washington DC. To Susan, and her stepson, Brian Sullivan, I owe the last "polishing" of the book. I appreciate this help greatly.

Finally I would like to thank my nuclear family: Shuli, my partner in life since we were adolescents ourselves, and our admirable grown-up sons, Adiel, Asaf, Eitan, Micha and Amitay – who never complained having to share their childhood and adolescence with our extended family – the children of Yemin Orde.

Chaim Peri

Foreword
by Micha Odenheimer

Like many good things in life the opportunity to help midwife this book came to me at just the right time, exactly as my children were entering the most challenging, outrageous period of adolescence. Fortunately for me, right when my teenage children's seemingly conscious strategy for turning me into a wounded, wrathful, raving shadow of my former self was increasing in sophistication and effectiveness, Dr. Chaim Peri initiated me into a new way of thinking about adolescence and parenting.

This was not my first meeting with Dr. Peri. In November 1990 I had traveled to Addis Ababa, the capital city of Ethiopia, to interview Mengistu Haile Mariam, the brutal and desperate dictator who held the fate of 25,000 Ethiopian Jews in his hands. Rebel forces were gaining ground in their drive to oust Mengistu, and in the muddy streets of Addis Ababa, undercurrents of ethnic and political violence coursed just below the barely controlled surface of daily life.

Israeli diplomats, doctors, and rescue workers flew in and out of the city, attending to the Ethiopian Jews who had evacuated their villages in the north and were now living in abject poverty as they awaited permission to emigrate. But what was an educator, the director of a near legendary youth village for teenagers in the north of Israel, doing in this harsh and unpredictable country?

The answer lay in the fact that Chaim, as he prefers to be known, conceived of the task of education in the broadest possible terms. Education is the process through which each generation becomes conscious of what is most essential, valuable and precious in life, and hands this legacy – human civilization itself, in all its possibility and power – to the next generation. The very act of taking responsibility, of attempting to influence historical events to the extent one is able, is, for Dr. Chaim Peri, inseparable from the educational task.

If the Ethiopian parents and siblings of teenagers living in Yemin Orde Village were trapped in an impossible situation because of the survival manipulations of a failing communist dictator, Chaim wanted to investigate and to fight for them. If the younger brothers and sisters of his teenage charges were dying of preventable diseases and malnutrition, Chaim had to try to change the situation. At the very least Chaim wanted see the situation with his own eyes and to keep a tide of consolation and hope flowing between the generations.

In the hilltop compound of the American Association for Ethiopian Jews (AAEJ), one of the Jewish organizations aiding the internal refugees, hundreds of men and women gathered in a dark, cavernous tent to see the photographs of their children, who had already emigrated to Israel, that Chaim had brought with him from Yemin Orde. Chaim carefully posted the photos on the canvas walls of the tent. As each parent located the image of his or her child, the tent, with its single light bulb, seemed to brighten with fresh radiance.

This was another lesson: no matter how far one journeys in the quest to mend the world, the relationship between parents and children is somehow always at the heart of the matter. Parenthood and education, in Chaim's teaching, are Siamese twins that cannot be separated. In order for education to succeed, it must be infused with the parental qualities of caring and emotional connection. And in order for parents to effectively rise to their task – and parenthood is always the challenge of a lifetime – they must become conscious of themselves as educators. Parents can draw strength and endurance from the knowledge that, in the eyes of their children, they hold the world in their hands. And in effect they do, because as parents, they have been entrusted with the charge of passing the secret of life and the flame of hope for a better world to the next generation.

The process through which this book emerged into the world occrred not in relective seclusion – during a sabbatical year or in the quiet of a library – but as life continued to froth and churn around Chaim. Initially, many of our meetings were held in Dr. Peri's office in the Village. Constant interruptions from young people, counselors and other staff forced us to seek other places to work. We talked and wrote in cafes, restaurants, lawyers' offices and hotel lobbies in Tel Aviv, Jerusalem, Atlit and Zichron Yaakov. And still the interruptions came fast and furious. A young person from the Village had gone missing for a few hours. A graduate – from a class that had matriculated five, ten or fifteen years before – might be having financial, career or marital problems. A group of orphans from the former Soviet Union, or the families of terror victims, or the children of foreign workers, had arrived at the Village. Dr. Peri's days and the life of Yemin Orde Youth Village were and are never routine.

As I listened to Chaim's stories of Yemin Orde graduates, and saw and heard first hand how their experiences in the Village were carved into their hearts. I spoke with many of the Village staff to see how the insights of Yemin Orde's methods had filtered into their consciousness. The lessons to be absorbed from the Village and its methods captivated my imagination. At the same time I pushed Chaim to make the book consciously address parents as its audience. As the father of a teenager I became convinced that Chaim's insight into adolescence and into parenthood could potentially help millions of parents around the world escape the cross-generational battle of egos and wills.

There is a story told about one of the great Jewish spiritual masters who noticed that one of his students, who was sitting with the rest of his disciples on a Sabbath eve, had a terrible pain in his eyes. As the others watched the master walked over and placed his hands over the eyes of the disciple, who was writhing in pain. Miraculously, the disciple's cries of pain ceased and his facial contortions were replaced by an expression of relief. Later, his friends demanded to know: had his pain really ceased at the touch of the teacher's hand?

"No," the disciple said, "the pain didn't go away. But it became a completely different kind of pain."

This book is not a manual that can magically change parents or adolescents, or the harsh realities of the world in which we have been charged with raising our children. But I believe that there is magic in the text – a deep and subtle magic that can shift our perspective and expand our consciousness so that parenting and educating becomes something different; the inherent pain involved transformed from the anguish of frustration to the comforting ache of growth. At its root this magic is the magic of faith – faith that no matter who we are, we have within ourselves what it takes to provide the guidance our children need in order to learn how to live in this world. It is the magic of faith in our teenagers and in the promise they carry within themselves, even at their most terrible moments. Ultimately, it is faith in the power of life.

Chapter 1
Adolescence

In Search of Parental Wholeness

This book is the story of a powerful belief in adolescence as an hour of grace. Not another "how to" guide in the face of parental despair, but a source of transformational insight into the reader's relationships with teenagers. By sharing my life experience I hope to re-ignite in my readers the will, ability and confidence to become our teenagers' guide and mentor.

My experience is grounded in Yemin Orde Wingate Youth Village in Israel, a residential educational community where I have served as director and head educator for nearly 30 years, and whose pulse of life provides the inspiration for this book. Yemin Orde Youth Village grew out of a need to provide a focal point for young souls wandering in the aftermath of historical ruptures and devastation, left void of parental guidance. Founded in 1953 in the fledgling state of Israel, the Village is named in honor of Orde Charles Wingate, the British Brigadier General who helped pioneering Jews establish the State of Israel.

Since its inception, this 77-acre Village on top of Mt. Carmel, just south of Haifa, has provided refuge to waves of children who have come to Israel in the aftermath of the convulsive upheavals of recent history. Most of the thousands of children and teenagers who arrived at this haven have experienced painful separations, their lives marred by heartbreaking family situations that left them confused and frustrated. These teenagers have been and remain my greatest teachers.

Some readers may ask, justifiably, whether lessons learned from teenagers coming from extreme circumstances apply to their children or students. I am convinced that the answer is yes. Contemporary conditions dictate that even in the most "normal" of homes, adult presence has been weakened, thus creating a void that has been filled with artificial substitutes for the real thing. The real thing is in us – those who gave life to the children, who brought them to this world, and those who feel responsible for them.

It is the quality of adult presence that can make a difference in adolescent lives. This is true no matter how privileged or how challenged these lives have been. For despite the prevalence of teenage rebellion and its implied rejection of our guidance, our youngsters want and need our presence. What I have learned at Yemin Orde is that even in the most unfavorable of circumstances we can raise children within an atmosphere of parental wholeness and offer them a bridge to a healthy and dynamic adulthood. I believe that if we can do it here, you can do it with your children, just about anywhere you may be.

Towards Different Attitudes

In contemporary society at the beginning of the 21st century many parents suffer from a lack of confidence in their ability to guide their children during the crucial years when they are becoming adults. Young people often angrily reject, so it seems, their parents' authority, values and ideals – or else sink into depression, anxiety or a slow burning, passive hostility. Parents feel wounded to the bone by what they perceive as their teenagers' disdain and impudence, or else feel a gnawing anxiety about their children's lack of passion, vitality and initiative.

Entire industries, notably tough-love military style schools and summer camps whose goal is to almost violently break down rebellious teenagers' resistance to adult discipline, have flourished over the last decades, exploiting parental confusion and despair.

The crisis of confidence regarding adolescents that today challenges many parents and educators is the result of the unraveling of traditional structures of meaning and community that have existed for thousands of years. The human psyche is hard-wired to find meaning in an existential context dense with interaction and cooperation between generations. Modern psychological theories, whose ideas have successfully penetrated our general culture, see human beings as motivated by instinctual drives, such as the sexual drive or by the ego's desire for autonomy and control. Although these drives and desires certainly exist, they offer at best a fragmentary view of what people really want. Human beings are first and foremost creatures who seek not sexual release or control and autonomy – however crucial these are – but human contact and the unfolding and realization of the fullness of their individual identity within the tapestry of social life.

Whether they know it consciously or not, children expect the generation that brought them into the world to transmit to them the secret of what it means to be a human being. When teenagers intuitively feel that they are not receiving this knowledge, which cannot be conveyed through words alone but must be given over by living example, they respond with inner disorder expressed in frustration, rebellion and anger.

The task of providing our children with the kind of example they seek sounds daunting, nearly impossible. The good news this book brings is that we can, through certain simple but immensely significant shifts of attitude and intent, provide our children with the taste and aura of wholeness and meaning that they so deeply need.

For earlier generations the centrality of the

relationship between parents and children could be taken for granted. When most of humanity lived in villages and tribal communities, surrounded by their extended family, a sense of coherence and meaning was woven into the natural flow of life. Children grew and developed within the aura of parental wholeness – meaning that parents and other significant adult figures radiated an emotionally coherent set of qualities, connections and values that anchored children within the human world of which they were becoming part.

The transformation of adolescence into a time sharply marked by intergenerational conflict coincides with the post-industrial era in the Western world, in which *the village* and all the communal values it embodies has been replaced by the predominance of urban life and the isolated nuclear family. That this reality should lead to a continuous cycle of irreconcilable rifts between generations is not something we need to accept as an immutable decree. Returning to the roots of human nature, in which children are raised within an aura of parental wholeness, is still a choice we can make, as the stories and the thoughts in the coming pages will show.

Over the years at Yemin Orde we have discovered that the possibility of offering parental wholeness to our children within the circumstances of our present world is not dependent on accumulating stores of knowledge or techniques, but on an inner state of mind that affects the way we view the task of parenting. Our aspiration to provide our children with what can honestly be regarded as parental guidance in a way that will genuinely resonate in the children's world brought us to search for an apparatus that could help reveal and activate that mssing quality of parental prescence in each of us.

Every Youngster Deserves a Mentor

A common mark of a confident adulthood is the decisive influence, during our own formative years, of a mentor. If we have had such an influence we are well aware of the difference it has made in our life. The mentor's impact is felt as much through his or her mere focus and presence as through the specific content of what he or she gives us. More than anything else, our mission is to proactively infuse our adolescent's world with the quality of presence that a mentor provides. What once may have been natural now requires conscious intention and some strategy.

Seemingly, the task of mentoring should be suited only for those adults who have "got it," who have the requisite charisma, stamina and conviction to produce the mentoring effect. My conviction is that every young person deserves a worthy mentor, and that all reasonably sound adults have the mentoring spirit within themselves, if they know where to search. It all begins with a quest for self-discovery, leading to the invisible center within our lives around which the fragments of our world can coalesce.

It Takes a Village. . .

Mentoring, I believe, begins with reconstructing the outline of the lost village of humankind within ourselves. The famous African proverb, "It takes a village to raise a child," which has been reintroduced into American consciousness through Hillary Rodham Clinton, reverberates with humankind's longing for this lost village.

We cannot return to the lost village. Would we really want to if we could? What we have is the privilege of using our awareness and insight to recreate, starting within ourselves, the "village state of mind" – reproducing through our own free choice and intention the sense of connection with others that is part of the anticipatory structure of human consciousness.

Our vision at Yemin Orde has been to ensure that behind each child is an educational community designed to reproduce the basic outline of humanity's lost village – a village that can instill in its children a recognition and pride in their past, a sense of direction and security about the future, an openness to transcendent values, a desire to improve communal reality, and a deeper understanding and insight regarding their weaknesses and strengths.

Is reconstructing the lost village within us an unrealizable task? For our many graduates, now successfully parenting their own children, reconstructing the village in their own hearts has proved attainable. They are the ones who convinced me that the principles we have discovered and activated while raising them in our Village of Yemin Orde are relevant and replicable in every home and for every parent.

What is left now is to share with you the essence of our experience, its foundations and its practical implications. We invite you to follow our story and find individual meaning in the human task of mentoring, thus inspiring a new generation capable of transforming the global village by infusing it with the contours and qualities of the original human village.

Chapter 2
The Lost Village of Humanity

Fragments of Parenting, Slivers of Love

My own experience as a child begins with the tragic years of the rise of Nazism and has a devastating absence at its center. I tell it because I believe that the energies and attitudes we bring to parenting have their origin in our own childhood. The deciphering of our childhood and teenage experiences is a central part of our inner lives no matter what stage of life we have reached. I wish to preface our discussion of the absent parent with an insight that has ripened in me since my teenage years: even the most devastating childhood wounds can be healed in adolescence.

My mother came to Israel, then ruled by the British, in the late 1930s at the age of 17. Her family had immigrated to Hanover, Germany in order to escape the grinding poverty and anti-Semitism of the Polish *shtetl*. Most of the Jews of Poland, including my mother's family, were Hasidim, devout followers of a mystical form of Judaism that emphasized community, ecstatic devotion and strict observance. In Germany Jewish immigrants from Poland were considered primitive by their more modern and secularized German Jewish counterparts. As immigrants without German citizenship or a supportive social network, they were especially vulnerable to Nazism.

The Nazis had already taken power and were beginning to reveal their cruelty when my mother left Germany, although few yet guessed the extent of the murderous depravity they intended. From the moment of her arrival in Palestine my mother attempted to obtain entry permits, called "certificates," so that her parents and

younger brother could join her in the land of Israel. She
stood in lines for countless hours, trying to navigate the
Byzantine bureaucracy of the British, whose main concern
was to prevent the mass immigration of Jews into the
country. To support herself my mother worked picking
oranges, cleaning houses, and caring for small children.
She met my father, an electrical engineer with his own story
of family separation and tragedy, and married him in 1940.

Soon she was pregnant with me. During the entire
course of her pregnancy my mother continued to clean
houses, and in her spare time redoubled her efforts to rescue
her family. By now the Germans had expelled them to a
refugee camp on the Polish border. She received a last
postcard from them, which I still have. In it her father
complains about her little brother, who in the crowded
camp has stopped studying Torah, the traditional term for
the Bible and other religious texts that Jews are commanded
to "meditate on morning and night." Instead, her father
writes, her brother has fashioned for himself a ball of rags
and plays games with it in the dirty alleys of the camp.

Near the end of her pregnancy, my mother became
ill with typhoid, and was weak when she gave birth to me
in September of 1941. The final blow to her sanity was the
news that her parents and brother had been murdered by
the Nazi machine, and that all her efforts to save them had
ended in failure. She had a mental breakdown, and was
admitted to a mental hospital. She was eventually released,
but she was never the same. She lived the rest of her life
alternating between mostly unsuccessful attempts to live a
normal life at home and periods of confinement in mental
institutions.

In light of these circumstances my father, who was
unable to raise me alone, placed me as a baby in an
institution for homeless children in Tel Aviv. I stayed there
until I myself almost died of typhoid when I was about

four years old. My grandmother, my father's mother, rescued me from this institution, and I lived with her off and on until I was six or seven, when I returned to my father and mother. They had divorced when I was four, but had reunited after a year. Although my father was only a distant presence as a parent, too sunk into his own thoughts and involved with his own life struggles to reach out emotionally to me, I have always admired the courage and integrity of his choice. Despite her suffering, depression and instability, he chose to live with my mother rather than abandon her.

My father fought in the 1948 War of Independence and took part in the Jewish conquest of Acre, an ancient seaport in northern Israel that filled up after the war with new Jewish immigrants, many of them Holocaust survivors. My father moved us there. One of the notable architectural features of Acre was a medieval castle located in the old city, which the British had used as a jail for political prisoners; some of the captured heroes of the Jewish resistance had been hanged there. The castle, which was surrounded by a moat that used to be filled with seawater, had been taken over by the new Israeli government and given to the Ministry of Health for use as an insane asylum. The castle-turned-asylum was located right across the street from my school. One of my childhood memories is seeing the castle through the window of my classroom, knowing my mother was interned inside. The high castle walls and the impassable moat symbolized for me the impossibility that I would ever have a normal childhood or a stable home.

Between periods of internment in the asylum, my mother was often melancholy. When her depression turned psychotic, I would sometimes have to chase after my half-dressed mother through the streets of town. I remember, at least once, actually bringing her to the asylum, where she was put into a room filled with other mentally ill people, men and women, Arabs and Jews. The asylum staff tended to treat the families as if they were extensions of the patients themselves. I felt as if the staff, the doctors, the very wards of the institution itself were trying to suck me into their midst, where I would disappear forever.

A mentally ill parent is for me the ultimate symbol of the kind of parent that the novelist Ian McEwan has found symptomatic of the 20th century – not fully present even when physically close. And yet my experience with my mother also taught me that fragments of good parenting, of love, are absorbed by children and can be built later into structures of wholeness. Even in the insanity of the household in which I was raised, I had some sort of compass. My mother would intermittently, in her brief periods free of psychosis or depression, show me samples of what true love meant. These were outbursts of normalcy that I could grasp, and it is impossible to exaggerate their importance. As I later learned, in my work as an educator, children can build whole worlds out of such slivers of parental love.

Still, it took me years to deal with my childhood, to make peace with it. It was a childhood where I did not have any model of parental wholeness. I could only see brokenness. And yet this shattering, this hole where the center should have been, sharpened my intuition, and gave me a sense, one might say, of what parental wholeness smells like, and has thus guided my career and the development of my educational thinking.

Adolescence – Its Absolute Formative Power

I began to recover from my childhood during my teenage years, through exposure to healthy parental figures and family environments that radiated wholeness – environments I was attracted to as a moth is to light. This experience planted within me the seeds of two important convictions.

The first is my belief in the absolutely formative power of adolescence no matter what was one's experience of childhood. One of Freud's important insights, among the most influential ideas of the 20th century, is his emphasis on the crucial impact of the early years of childhood on people's emotional development. Swayed by Freud, educators such as A. S. Neil, founder of the Summerhill School and one of the spiritual fathers of the experimental and democratic school movement, believed that a child's psychological makeup could not be radically altered after the age of seven or eight.

Without diminishing the significance of the early childhood years, the conviction that the teenage years are equally momentous in their shaping power has been the beacon of my educational approach. Although the seeds of this conviction were sown through my own experience growing up, I have had this belief confirmed over and over again during my years of working with teenagers who were able, during adolescence, to heal childhood traumas and change the trajectory of their lives. If I could tell one thing to every parent and educator, it would be that every hour of the teenage years is precious, each experience as potent in its capability to heal or to wound as countless hours of childhood.

The other belief I bring with me from my adolescence is that parental figures are no less crucial to teenagers than they are to infants, although in a different way. We know that infants need constant care. Although it is less obvious, this is equally true for adolescents. This is a truth that is easy to miss, since a struggle to be independent and an urge to rebel also characterize the teenage years. But adolescents need a very specific kind of parental presence. Their encompassing need is for us to radiate an aura of wholeness amidst the chaos they experience both in the world and within their own fragmented psyche – a chaos they often embody and express in outbursts directed at us. This may seem an amorphous and impenetrable task, but, as I hope to show, it is indeed an attainable goal.

Future Memories – Future Psyche

One way to reflect on these insights – the formative nature of adolescence and the adolescent thirst for their parents' presence in their lives – is to recognize and grasp that we bear responsibility for our children's future memories. Our inner life continues to be profoundly connected to our experiences in childhood and adolescence for as long as we live. For much of the rest of our lives we are engaged in remembering and deciphering our early years, which adolescence crowns and seals. Our relationship with our children is thus a seeding for the future. The nature and quality of the moments in our relationship that repeat themselves over and over eventually crystallize into the inner structure of our children's future psyche.

Looking back on our childhood and adolescence, we tend to think that our psyche was deeply influenced by dramatic or extraordinary events. But in the end, it is the mundane and the everyday that becomes ingrained in us, forming the emotional and cognitive patterns of our personality. The dramatic events we remember can be compared to the pictures in our childhood albums, frozen in time. These photos evoke emotions and associations far beyond what the picture would mean to another observer. Those almost indescribable feelings, which the photograph cannot portray, are what has truly stayed with us from those times, not the frozen split second of the photo. I have often thought about how different the narratives of countless children's lives would be if their parents had acted with the awareness that they were writing, day by day, the memories that would stay with their children forever.

At times, while attending weddings or other joyous events of alumni, shreds of memory, images from their adolescence, burst into my mind in sharp contrast to the uplifting occasion. Whenever this happens, I re-experience the sometimes horrendous incidents of the past. Strangely enough, at times like these I am overwhelmed by a triumphant sense that the incredible healing power of adolescence has proven itself once again. It is my wish that you will eventually taste a similar sense of triumph at the end of the lengthy path you will travel with the adolescents that are part of your life.

Chapter Three

Yemin Orde Youth Village

The Flow of Life

Founded in the early 1950s, soon after the birth of the State of Israel, Yemin Orde Youth Village, like Israel itself, has been a crucible in which children from tiny Ethiopian villages far removed from Western civilization have found themselves living alongside children from Tel Aviv, London, Moscow and Paris. Teens whose childhood was marred by traumas and who have wounds of almost indescribable severity have struggled, rebelled and finally flourished alongside children from intact families and middle class backgrounds.

Yemin Orde is located on a peak in the Carmel Mountain range overlooking the Mediterranean Sea. Below our Village is historic Ein Hod, a famous artists' colony. From a bird's eye view someone looking at Yemin Orde would see a forest of pine trees, cypress and cedar around its periphery, and a series of white buildings with red tile roofs. Along with cottages where 30 families of staff live, there are classrooms, a synagogue, a glass-walled dining hall, a modern art center, a small library, two computer centers, twenty children's homes housing more than 500 children, and assorted other structures. The campus itself, although surrounded by a fence for security reasons, can easily be breached by the ingenuity of teenagers, who are often talented escape artists.

One of the first questions that many visitors to Yemin Orde ask me is whether I have trouble with children attempting to "escape" the school, i.e. going AWOL. After all, Haifa and its malls are nearby, and the beach is so tantalizingly close that it can be seen from the Western edge of the campus. With 500 children in residence at any given time, one might expect a certain percentage to desert.

On the whole, however, this does not happen. Although rebellion, protest and other forms of anger directed at authority are a regular and expected part of teenage development here, running away is not. This is not because our Village is a teenager's idea of paradise. Rather, teenagers stay in Yemin Orde because they sense that the adults sharing their lives convey a sense of purpose – a road map which can guide them forward. The absence of this kind of road map in the crucial, formative years of adolescence, even in the best case, invites a search for answers through various therapies and psychological theories, in accordance with the current trends.

Hidden Sources of Strength

Being an educator means learning from your students all the time. In my case it has afforded me the chance to learn from many kind of stories and experiences of adolescence, emanating from vastly different locations and cultures. Perhaps none has affected me as deeply as the story of the Ethiopian Jewish youngsters who began to arrive in Yemin Orde in the fall of 1981. Contemplating these youngsters and their hidden sources of strength reawakened and reinforced the lessons I had learned in my own childhood about the resilience of adolescence and the thirst for parental presence.

The first Ethiopian teenagers who arrived in Yemin Orde in 1981 were newcomers not only to the village, but also to Israel. They were part of the first trickle in what would become, over the next decade, a wave of new immigrants from war-torn Ethiopia, and they composed the first mass emigration of a Jewish tribe from East Africa to Israel. This immigration confronted us with a virtually unprecedented phenomenon in the history of mankind: the nearly instantaneous passage of a whole community whose way of life had not changed for thousands of years to a hyper-modern state where they arrived as full citizens.

The Ethiopians stood out from the other teenagers by virtue of their skin color, and also because they were heirs to an ancient Jewish tradition with its own unique customs and religious interpretations that differed from every other Jewish community in the world. But what was extraordinary to me about these youngsters was not color or even their fascinating traditions. It was the route that they had taken to reach Israel. Despite constant peril to their lives, most of these youngsters had walked through hundreds of miles of bandit-infested mountains and deserts in order to make it out of Communist Ethiopia to Sudan, where a route to the Promised Land had tenuously and perilously opened up.

Traveling in groups where the teenagers often outnumbered the adults, these youngsters had braved hunger, thirst, disease, outlaws, wild animals and the fury of government soldiers who considered their exodus a betrayal. Virtually all these teenagers had witnessed deaths of close relatives, including siblings, parents or grandparents, at some point on their voyage. Often, they themselves had been close to death during the course of their journeys, because of starvation, illness or external threat.

And yet, although the traumas they experienced remained etched in their memories, these young people mainly recalled the exuberance and stamina that had lifted them across the wilderness, as if they were ships whose sails had been filled by their own mighty spirits. I knew that if I could find a way to help them tap that amazing spirit again, it could propel them across the next chasm they would have to navigate. Within a short period of months, they had to follow a track that had taken a much of civilization hundreds of years to cross.

Inner Road Map

Where, in fact, were these teenagers coming from if not from the lost village of humanity, which had survived in Ethiopia, the cradle of human civilization, into the 21st century? It was the rural African village – familial and enveloping, a social structure that had capably sustained and transmitted its values to generation after generation of its children – that was the source of their strength. What we in the West had lost over the course of the last several hundred years, they stood to lose nearly instantly in their transition to the new world of mass culture and alienating cities in the West. I would learn, however, that the values and the sustenance which the village transmitted can be retained by the human heart long after geographical and historical borders had been left behind.

Eighteen years later, in the winter of 1999, I found myself reflecting again on the astonishingly resourceful spirit concealed in seemingly average adolescents. I was in Chuntra, a youth village in a region of northern India where hundreds of adolescent refugees from Chinese-occupied Tibet had found a new home. I had traveled to India as part of a continuing dialogue with Tibetan educators that would eventually bring Tibetan youngsters to study at Yemin Orde in Israel. Many of the refugees in Chuntra were children who had fled a world shattered by the Chinese assault on Tibetan cultural and religious life. In order to find a new life they were forced to uproot themselves from their friends and family.

As I listened to these young Tibetans tell their stories, the ordeals they had endured came alive in my imagination. I could see these children making their way on foot through treacherous mountain passes. I could see the fear in their young faces as they thought they heard the voices of a Chinese army patrol coming towards them from around a bend, and their joy and relief when such dangers proved unfounded. I could see them building a campfire in the cold night air, eating a meager meal with a sense of gratitude for whatever they had managed to find. I could almost taste their tears, as they lay wrapped in their blankets, thinking about the family they had left behind and might never see again. I could also imagine the excitement on their faces as they crossed into India on their way to the new life for which they had sacrificed so much.

As I sat in the shadow of the Himalayan Mountains, the unfamiliar smell of Tibetan cooking spices wafting in from another room, I was reminded of the Ethiopian children whose path through a different kind of wilderness was really so similar. Like the Tibetans, they had endured a terrible ordeal. What was even more powerful than the conjunction of external circumstances was the inner similarity of these teenagers – Ethiopian Jewish and Tibetan. Both had displayed enormous resilience and vitality in the face of danger, hardship and the threat of death. Like migratory birds on their epoch flights across oceans and continents, these teenagers had been able to marshal all their powers in a nearly superhuman effort.

From where had they drawn this strength? It seemed obvious that it was their clarity of purpose that gave them so much inner power. I could detect a tremendous drive towards life in the Tibetan and Ethiopian children, a zest for the possibilities offered by the new kind of existence that lay just over the ridge, past the next snowdrift, or just beyond the border. The Tibetan teenagers, too, stood to lose the web of meaning that had nourished them during their childhood – the fast disappearing traditional human village. Yet perhaps this "village state of mind," cultivated over so many thousands of years and hundreds of generations, lives inside each of us as a potential awaiting activation.

On the face of it the strength and vitality of the Ethiopian and Tibetan children would seem to have little to do with parental presence. After all, many of the Ethiopian and Tibetan teens whose stories amazed me did not have parents with them on their near-impossible journeys. Yet a feeling of being guided by the generation that brought them into the world is something children absorb so deeply that it transcends physical presence. Children and teenagers can draw from the aura of parental presence no matter where they are. Both groups of teenagers drew their strength from the knowledge that in attempting their journey, they were fulfilling the deepest dreams and aspirations of their ancestors. These dreams functioned like an inner road map. They marked the final destination of the journey in bold colors, and fixed within the psyche of each child his personal connection to the journey.

To grow up in an Ethiopian Jewish village – where every older person was empowered with parental authority and charged with a parental role in relation to the village's children – meant being exposed every single day to the communal dream of returning to Jerusalem.

"If we did a good deed, or fulfilled a task well," an elder might say to us, " 'I bless you to return to our land,' meaning Zion, Jerusalem," said Negiste, who was 14 years old when she set out for Sudan. The journey to Jerusalem, via Sudan, was thus an adventure into the unknown, shielded, supported and inspired by values that the children had absorbed into their own identity since birth.

The Tibetan children also came from a community in which the mundane events and interactions with parents and elders served as a loom on which ancient traditions and future hopes were woven each day into a tapestry of meaning. The flight from Chinese-occupied Tibet was a flight to the Dalai Lama exiled in India and the autonomous Tibetan culture he represented. The incalculable value of this culture was an axiom, part of the air that surrounded the children as they moved through the village environment, an axiom that was the covert subtext of all their encounters with parents, teachers and elders.

These groups of African and Asian adolescents thus moved through a world that had been given over to them by an older generation that had collectively raised them since the moment of their birth. It was a world whose meaning and direction were mediated by tangible parental figures. The convictions and values of the elders were conveyed to the children on a bridge created by the relationship between the generations.

The youngsters moving through deserts, jungles and snowy mountain passes might have appeared as if they were alone, but they were not. They carried the imprint of their parents' spirit inside of them. Reconstituting that spirit and allowing parental guidance a central place within the relationship between generations, it seemed to me, would bring us a long way towards reclaiming our birthright — the lost village of humanity.

Chapter Four
A Village – A Community

Village of Humanity

What is it that transforms a group of individuals into a community? Often, in Yemin Orde Youth Village, it is the intrinsic drive for justice that has galvanized our youngsters into an active community. Community activism is forged through the sense of the suffering of others and identification with their existing situation, and thus a feeling of participation in a shared fate.

When our graduates look back on their years in our Village, the motif that surfaces over and over is the way their communal experience at Yemin Orde compensated for their bitter lack of family and stable surroundings that they had suffered during childhood. The weakening of the family and sense of community in general today increases the urgency of introducing communal qualities into our schools.

Indeed, for some time now the issue of community has been an important item on the agenda of educators. There has been much lip service paid to the notion that violence, drugs and other problems plaguing many public schools can be combated by creating a more intense sense of community.

Unfortunately, for the most part, the talk has remained talk – a flag without much wind behind it. Flags that decorate our offices or auditoriums sometimes find their way into the foreground, during communal celebrations and in the aftermath of crises such as that which the United States experienced on September 11, 2001.

The flag then is a representation of the best in ourselves and in the community-at-large, a symbol pointing upwards around which we can all rally. The teenage years are in some sense like a period of sturm and drang, in which the stability achieved during childhood is no longer sufficient for daily life, and new threats make the future into a frightening unknown. Flags create a point around which people can gather in times of distress and celebration in order to create collective strength, which in turn lends them security as individuals. The intensity of adolescence mandates that we fly flags for them all the time, rather than keep them in the background as a static reminder of glory.

When there is no ideological glue or intensive parental involvement binding a school together, community feeling is difficult to produce. This is true especially in large public schools whose students and their parents may have little in common except for geographical proximity. When we are talking about children from impoverished inner-city homes, or homes haunted by a feeling of failure, creating community is even harder due to the feelings of isolation and alienation with which many of these children have been raised. Their family's daily struggle for survival often left little energy to devote to communal affairs, and little faith in the power of association to strengthen and enrich individual lives.

Only if a school's desire to create community has the urgency of an existential need do efforts to reach this goal stand a chance of success. In Yemin Orde, despite the weak jumping off point of many of our youths and the eclectic backgrounds from which they came, we have been able to create a strong communal bond. This success is attributable, first and foremost, to our commitment to the centrality of community as a human and educational goal. True community cannot be a by-product of something else. Although any group that comes together for a unified purpose may take on aspects of a community; a community is alive only if on some core level its life is its purpose.

No matter what lofty purposes a human being is devoted to, in order to be strong and healthy, one needs to feel, at some deep foundational level, a simple joy at being alive. The same is true in terms of community; a school or other group may have many goals, but the impulse to community must be a vibrant force at the core of that school or group's life else it be perceived, rightly, as an empty motto. Transformation of the institution into community can only come through the metamorphosis, or even the intention of metamorphosis, of at least a skeleton staff consisting of people willing to participate in the adventure of preparedness, which entails changing within.

Transforming schools into communities is important not only because doing so will bring down the level of violence and substance abuse, although it undoubtedly will, it is important because our adolescents must learn what it is to participate in the life of a community. As a society, we cannot afford to produce communal cripples, people for whom isolation, anonymity and alienation are the norm. Our teenagers must emerge from their adolescent years having found an expression for the natural human urge for belonging. The taste of community that children experience during their adolescent years will whet their appetite to participate in communal life for the remainder of their lives.

Perpetually Reinvented Community

One of the outstanding educators of the last century was Kurt Hahn. Born in Germany, he continued his work in England after Hitler's rise to power. I was personally introduced to his work by his sister-in-law, Lola Hahn Wahrburg, who devoted her life to saving Jewish children from the clutches of the Nazis and rehabilitating child survivors after the Holocaust. Towards the end of her long life she saw in Yemin Orde a continuation of her brother-in-law's educational path.

Kurt Hahn believed that the schools of the future must function as communities of meaning and idealism in which the drive towards self-realization is harnessed to an overarching goal: the creation of a better world. A dynamo of ideas and activities, Hahn's fecund mind produced an array of educational initiatives, including an international network of schools called the United World Colleges, and the short course designed to catalyze teenage transformation, Outward Bound. Hahn mostly focused on influencing and training the children of the elite in the hopes that they would later be in positions through which they could profoundly affect positive changes in society. In Yemin Orde we have applied Hahn's idea of schools as communities of meaning to the raising of children from impoverished backgrounds and dysfunctional families.

One important principle to keep in mind is that, especially for adolescents, community is something that has to be created over and over again. Dedication to and identification with a particular community is strongest among its founders. Here in Israel we've witnessed this phenomenon in regards to the *kibbutz* movement. During the half century preceding the founding of the State, and for a decade or so afterwards, hundreds of *Kibbutzim* – collective farms, with their own schools, economy, culture and welfare system – were carved out of barren deserts and swamps. The founding members of the *kibbutz* endured enormous hardships in order to establish these communities against all odds. Often they lived under conditions of dire poverty. Ultimately, most of the *kibbutzim* thrived, and contributed enormously to the development of Israel while creating culturally vibrant and ideologically committed communities. But lo and behold, the second and third generation of Israelis born on *kibbutz* began a mass exodus from *kibbutz* life, despite having achieved a far higher standard of living than their parents or grandparents had ever dreamed possible.

One of the clear lessons that emerged was that the farther removed people were from having been present at the *kibbutz's* founding, the less connected they felt to the *kibbutz* as individuals. Since they did not feel like founders, the emphasis on community was interpreted as coming at the expense of individual expression. In order to feel that they were living their own life many left the *kibbutz* to live in cities.

Perhaps for similar reasons, the Torah tells us that all the souls of Israel, including those of the unborn generations to come, were present at Mount Sinai, when Israel became a community. True membership always means partaking in the moment of origins in some way.

Schools that want to be communities should take this lesson seriously. Instead of giving new students the feeling that they are joining an already established community, the school should aspire to be a community forever in formation, fundamentally changed by each new member. Every child at his or her point of entry, it should be assumed, is far from being part of a community. Especially when talking about those who are people emerging from a traumatic childhood, teenagers are creatures deeply absorbed in themselves. One cannot look at community as something static, as if you are adding new individuals to something that already exists, because with that mindset, the children and the community will repel each other.

With each class, it is necessary to build the consciousness of community anew. In Hebrew the word for education is "dedication" or "inauguration." If the educator does not believe that he or she is inaugurating something new, then education is not really happening. In education we are always beginning – the fruits are always later. Initiating youngsters into the passionate desire for community can be accomplished only by engaging them as individuals, allowing them to feel that the magical power of the collective could not have been conjured without the potency of their unique presence.

Community – In the Service of Ego

Most youngsters arrive in our Village with the experience of having felt weakened by the group to which they belong. They may have suffered from or internalized stereotypes that were tagged onto them as children of immigrants or single parent families, or residents in distressed, low-income neighborhoods. In order to change their concept of belonging, to open them up to community, we have to turn this notion upside down. We have to make our teenagers feel empowered by their membership in the group – empowered not as part of the group, but *as individuals* because of the group. In short, we need to create a synergy in which the group is continuously felt to be drawing its power from the individual potencies of its participants, even as it bestows upon them the blessings of its collective power.

For us at Yemin Orde the presence of alumni is a key factor in demonstrating the power the community possesses to change the lives of individuals for the better. From their first days in our Village, teenagers know that the Yemin Orde community is not an artificial construct governed by the abstract set of rules that determine that high school lasts for four years. We continually reiterate that membership in our Village community does not dissipate suddenly the day after graduation. Alumni remain part of the day to day life of the Village. Our youngsters know the extent to which the Yemin Orde community and the alumni continue to give to each other synergistically long after graduation. The alumni share their lives as they pass through the army, through university, into marriage, and as they are creating their own family.

Those who have succeeded share both the joy and the resources that are the result of their success with the Village adolescents. Conversely, the Village continues to help alumni, both financially and with our name and connections, to the best of our abilities, in furthering their education, helping them get work and generally succeeding along the path they have chosen.

The role of alumni in reinforcing a sense of community is recognized and utilized in schools such as Harvard and Yale, Eton and Exeter. Generations of highly prominent and well connected alumni keep in close contact with the school and serve to keep us aware of its elite nature and the expected successes of its graduates. The innovation of Yemin Orde, which we believe deserves adoption on a much broader scale, is to make alumni a significant matter of concern and activity for schools that serve weaker populations.

When the youth in our Village see alumni returning to celebrate their wedding, graduation from university or attainment of the rank of officer in the army, they understand the role of community in changing the course of individual lives. It is high time that school systems serving 'weak' populations consider their intensive, continual contact with graduates as a program that was first and foremost designed to help their current student population. What if inner-city schools had continuous, built-in programs that served alumni by helping them to obtain scholarships, counseling them about career choices, helping them to find work, celebrating their achievements and smoothing out their failures? These efforts, even if kept on a low flame for lack of resources, would go a long way towards creating an authentic sense of community at the school, as well as creating trustworthy models of hope and fulfillment for the future. It is our experience that the investment of time, funding and energy that such a program entails will eventually be justified by the quality of human lives it fosters as well as its quantitative economic returns.

One strategy for enhancing awareness of the advantages of membership in a community is to consciously create a broader network of people with whom the school is associated. Our Village has a number of "adopted" parents and grandparents, older figures who represent stability, wisdom and connections to the higher strata of Israeli society.

Rachel Rabin, the martyred Prime Minister's sister and one of the early founders of *Kibbutz Manara* on the Lebanese border, is an occasional visitor to our Village. So are artists, architects, businesspeople and other public figures. Our youngsters absorb that their Village has a network of people that care about them and the Village, and that can be a resource later in life, when possible and appropriate. This strategy can be used successfully by any school. At its core, it sends the message that belonging is not a prison but rather a springboard through which one can reach wider and wider circles of affiliation.

Struggles provide an ideal context in which individuals can perceive their own powers emerge as they participate in communal efforts. Schools constantly need to make efforts, against all odds, to attain more resources, better funding, the expansion of facilities or the creation of opportunities for their alumni. Instead of hiding these struggles, students should be made to feel part of them, as if they personally have a stake in the outcomes.

Last summer, a group of our youngsters were not paid as they had been promised for jobs they had completed. Yemin Orde took up their cause, and after several rounds of letters, phone calls, and threats of legal action, we managed to help them recover their wages. Just as importantly, we let the other young people know exactly what we were doing all the way through, including them in the excitement of the battle and reminding them of the extra value-added of being part of a community.

Chapter Five

Routine and Bureaucracy

Enemies of Community

Where it is possible, schools should seek opportunities to fight for causes that are consistent with their ideology and stand a chance of galvanizing the student population. We can think of it as another form of team sports, with the stakes not winning games, but changing reality. And just as team sports are opportunities for individual talents and willpower to shine, so are public campaigns. However, there is one most important difference: the battles in which the school engages must be real.

How far we have drifted from the original experience of life in rural villages can be measured by our belief that education can take place in a protected bubble in which words and simulation are the primary educational tool. One cannot establish and reinforce community through simulation. To what extent do adolescents perceive the struggle we wish to involve them in as real and not masturbatory? To that extent will the process of struggle be able to engage their inner powers and awaken their sense of belonging?

This, incidentally, is the secret to creating a community that is always in the process of being created, so that every teen feels close to the origins. One must consciously allow the facade of stability that institutions work so hard to put in place to be knocked out of whack, at least a little bit. Of course, this approach must be balanced by the reassurance that things will turn out all right in the end – adolescents should ultimately live with a feeling of protection rather than existential threat. But disturbing balances and asking teenagers to help influence a situation in which the stakes are real is a crucial step in awakening their hidden powers.

Routine is the enemy of community, especially where adolescents are concerned. Adolescence is so short, and we have such a small amount of time, as educators or parents, in which to convey the essence of belonging to our children. If they do not experience the rhythm of community as a pulse of life, as something with its own urgencies and surprises, they will retreat into their own private world. Or into the world of their peers, fed by a subculture that feels exciting because it appears to be constantly under threat. Only by continuously raising flags, fighting, struggling, and challenging the status quo can a community avoid ossification and deadening.

Bureaucracy is thus the other great foe of community. Where one is strong, the other has no real foothold. To whatever extent possible bureaucracy should be reduced or eliminated. To the extent it cannot be, then both its procedures and its logic should be made transparent. Adolescents should be taught the reasons that we have forms, procedures and hierarchies so that they understand that bureaucracy, where it must exist, is not a matter of principle but of function – that it serves community, rather than the other way around.

Accessible Authority

This attitude towards bureaucracy should be built into the physical environment of schools. The architecture of schools, particularly their physical layouts, can serve to either magnify or reduce alienation and fear. In our Village there is no main administration building. The administrative operations needed to run each section are carried out in the area itself, as part of everyday life. When there is a separate administration building that concentrates much of the institution's power in one location, this broadcasts a kind of "Big Brother" image, as if the administrators are organizing life without being part of life. It is important that the administration participates in the flow of life, and that children clearly see this.

There are many schools where the headmaster or director is reachable only by navigating a long hall and then making it past the barricade of a secretary's office. Instead, educators should be cultivating accessibility by creating an environment of availability. Everything about the architecture of the school and the placement of offices should encourage openness and convey a sense of transparency. Youngsters in our Village learn soon after arriving that even when I am in a meeting, and the secretary is unwilling to interrupt me, they have recourse if they really need to see me. They can walk around the back of my office and knock on the window. Besides concretely demonstrating that my intention is to remain as accessible to them as possible, the back-window knock shows that, in our community, relationship takes precedence over rules.

Formalities exist, but when the emotional intimacy that nourishes community is present, there is always a back way around them. This also serves to reinforce the youngsters' moral judgment at a very crucial juncture in their development. Although rules and laws are generally to be followed, one's judgment is relevant in assessing their validity in cases where they seem to conflict with urgent human values – in this case, the preference of relationship over administrative rigidity.

Authority that is inaccessible, on the other hand, is an enemy of community through its reinforcement of a fear of separation and abandonment. Teenagers need to feel that the people who hold power in their lives can be reached without formality or delay. Teenagers should ideally be able to talk to their counselors, educators, and the director of the Village without an appointment when necessary, and about whatever they wish to discuss.

We have learned over the years to try to use our youngsters' requests and desires as educational opportunities. Kids, of course, do not need to get everything they ask for. Parents and educators can say no, or the request can become part of a more complicated negotiation. But even if the final answer is no, the fact that the child has had the chance to discuss the request is of tremendous significance, even if what we see is only disappointment. This opportunity should be built into the environment. In the short-term, the youngster engages in an intimate discourse rather than being thrown back against a wall of frustration. The long lasting fruit is the creation of a personality able to make demands on itself, provided the young person has good reason to see the adult authority as encircled together with him or her in an extended sense of self.

The effort to include adolescent representation in the leadership of the school must be real or it will only increase feelings of distrust in light of the gap between statement and actual partnership. Such representatives should be allowed to understand school politics and finances, and when there are problems, even scandals, they should hear about it. It is amazing to see how our board members take on the role of educators due to the presence of our adolescents at meetings.

When the Village's accountants share and explain documents to our youngsters, they create a different kind of attitude to our organization, property and financial commitments. This attitude is one of inner coherence between our administrative operations and our educational goals, and it is something we seek to transmit to even the newest youngster arriving in our Village. We also want the children to be able to understand that administrators are not invulnerable, and are prone to error and possibly even misdeed. We want them to be able to talk about the personalities involved in institutional politics, because those murky crosscurrents created when discussion flows into gossip, like salty and fresh water in an estuary, produce the lifeblood of communal feeling.

We do not want anyone in the school or the administration to be a placard, known only by his or her function. Secretaries, educators, cooks and administrators all have to have a human face. We want our Village to be the repudiation of Kafka's universe of alienation. This means that the community, including the children, needs to have some window into the intimacy of our staff – their past, problems and challenges. I make a practice of taking new youngsters at our Village on a tour of my house, showing them at least a small opening into the inner dimensions of my life. Then, even when I am acting in my role as director, they feel that they can see at least a little bit beyond that role into the totality of my life.

Clandestine Arteries and Stopping Life

It is people who create community. If schools are serious about this task then the heads of the system must value and honor not only those educators who bring academic excellence and honors to the school, but also those few people who are agents of unity and community. For they are as important and significant as are the great teachers of math. They are agents of community feeling within the system, and just as all sorts of knowledge and information and gossip flows through the system in an informal way, so can communality, if these agents exist.

Similarly, the presence of alumni, as in the case of Yemin Orde, provides a connective tissue linking teenagers and their teaching and administrative staff.

We have an opportunity to use the same currents

that carry gossip and news of scandal as a channel to infuse the system with a feeling of community, but we must make a conscious effort to do so. The opened windows of intimacy weaken the need for a separate youth subculture based on categorical disdain for the world of adults. Our goal should be to bring the culture and subculture of the school closer together, so that a single network of arteries carries the buzz of information and gossip to the community as a whole, as if it were one body. Communities must suffer the bad as well as celebrate the good.

Recently, two of our beloved teachers died of cancer within a single year. Not long afterwards, the eight year-old daughter of one of our Village's central educational figures was murdered in a terrorist attack. A feeling that our Village was under the sway of some kind of curse engulfed all of us. The reverse has also happened, where a string of awards and outstanding successes of our graduates creates a wave of communal uplifting of which every individual feels a part.

Along with these informal arteries, whose significance cannot be exaggerated, we have created other channels for disseminating information. Chief among these is the Village's cable television channel, which broadcasts roughly edited personal stories, alumni success stories, and the stories of our ongoing struggles, as well as birthdays and other information, all to underscore and emphasize the synergetic interplay between community and the individual.

Misdeeds, and the shame they may produce, can be another powerful force for constituting community. At Yemin Orde, whenever there is an event that shames us, violence or threat, for example, we stop life. We do not let things go on as usual, and routine is broken. The music playing on the Village loudspeakers in the dining hall is silenced. Even classes are interrupted. Because we are a community, because we are all connected and because something has happened that negates the essence of community, life cannot go on as usual. Just as on television, "breaking news" interrupts the regularly scheduled programs.

Several years ago, a video player was stolen from one of the Village common rooms. I immediately stopped classes and cancelled all extracurricular activities. We organized the young people into discussion groups and explained that life in the Village would not resume as normal until the crisis in trust that the theft of public property had created was resolved. After several hours, a note was found in the synagogue, posted on the most sacred space in the Village, the Holy Ark where the Torahs are stored. The note gave instructions that led to the recovery of the video player in a city a hundred miles to the south of our Village.

Many times the communal atmosphere created in response to a "crime" can lead to its solution. For the "thief" listening in as a respected member of the Village community to discussions about various aspects of what may have led our anonymous perpetrator to engage in such an act, helped that youth to reflect on the deed from a different perspective. The youngster was able to see the 'crime' as an aberration of his or her substantive and permanent identity as a member of the Yemin Orde community.

In taking measures that stop the normal flow of life, I hope to create a memory and understanding that will last for the rest of our teenagers' lives.

"Were you ever in a place where there was violence?" I hear a voice asking one of our teens later in life.

"Yes, I was. And life stopped, because I was in a community, and communities cannot tolerate violence."

The message I want to convey is that as long as we

act as a community, the flow of life in our Village continues. But when the intrinsic norms without which a community cannot exist are disturbed, an emergency is declared, almost as if life itself had been threatened.

As in every instance, judgment must be exercised in this regard. Sometimes, stopping the life of the community is what a teenager intends with his or her outrageous or threatening behavior. One of our teens once attempted to hang herself from the branch of a tree, although at a time and in a manner that insured that she would be cut down in time. An event as serious as this might warrant stopping the flow of life, but in this case I judged that it would also feed this young woman's feeling that self-destructive acts were the best way to get the attention of the entire community focused on her.

Part of what creates a community is its relationship to other communities or groups. A community has to have an extended sense of belonging. That which binds us to each other also binds us to others outside our immediate group, and these widening circles of identification reinforce our primary communal identity. Yemin Orde identifies with all groups whose values are humanistic, and who combine an authentic interest in holiness or spirituality with a commitment to pluralism. And yet we are still a community unto ourselves. By learning to distinguish between various shades and forms of group identity, our teens hone on the subtleties of communal feeling.

Serving as a host for other groups is also a way of strengthening community. Throughout the year our Village hosts an array of guests, from the families of terror victims, to the children of foreign workers, to disabled children and their families. Being a host for others is a complementary form of raising group consciousness of struggling together against outside forces. It is group identity forged by creating porous borders through giving.

Chapter Six

The Belly of Jonah's Whale

As part of reconstructing an inner sense of home for our children, we have scattered womb-like structures throughout the Village where small groups of children can sit together and talk in their native language. Our "wombs" are round shacks made of wood and branches in which we have hung enlarged photos depicting everyday life in the lands they have left behind. Our aim and hope is that every time youngsters gather in these spaces they step out with slightly more insight into themselves and the processes they are going through than when they entered.

Among the staff we have given this experience the code name *Jonah's Whale,* thus attributing a broader significance and context to the natural urge of the children to group together in an intimacy whose contours they themselves have chosen. In our tradition the whale that swallows Jonah as he attempts to escape from his mission and destiny becomes a refuge for incubating insight and energies that later enable him to save the entire civilization of Nineveh. The formation of youth subculture groups can too often and too easily take a destructive course, largely because the inarticulate, threatened response of adults becomes a self-fulfilling prophecy. By making an effort to transform our attitude we can forestall this negative result. We can create a genuinely positive association, even when we feel worried or threatened by our teenager's modes of bonding to peers. This will assure us a place in the picture instead of guaranteeing our expulsion.

I am reminded of one particular group of teenage immigrants from several Middle Eastern countries who used their sessions in the womb-like havens to talk about their future. Like other teenagers they used their seclusion to express themselves in ways they were uncomfortable doing in the clear light of day. This might well include smoking, using rough language and analyzing the virtues of the opposite sex. Yet the context of *Jonah's Whale*, which floated in the air in relation to the youngsters' "havens," ultimately transformed these places into breeding grounds for idealistic musings about the future a la *Dead Poets Society.*

As in the Biblical story of Jonah, they emerged from regressive confinement in a dark place with a new trajectory, if not a sense of mission. In the end, romanticizing and fantasizing in the warm darkness about a bright future turned into an actual plan. Impressed by their resolve to try to create a future together and their desire to learn more about life in Israel, we arranged to travel with them to the Galilee. At some point in our journeying we reached a hilltop near Nazareth that was now abandoned, although two shelters and several wooden shacks still remained from a previous attempt at settlement. Why had the buildings been abandoned? Could another group of people succeed in bringing life to this hilltop? A fiery discussion erupted.

"Why not?" they exclaimed, "Test us! We will make a paradise out of this place! One day we will bring our parents to live with us here."

I clearly remember Yossi, one of the teens, pointing to a clump of rocks, and saying, "That's where the bank is going to be."

"And over there," said Benny, "the movie theatre is going to stand."

Almost twenty years later, in a PBS documentary about Yemin Orde, some of these same graduates were interviewed in their beautiful homes on that same hilltop, as their own children played around them. They had succeeded beyond my hopes. Today, Hoshayah, the community they founded, is a thriving village of 250 well-established families. Reminiscing about the founding of Hoshayah, the graduates retrospectively attribute their ability to turn a desolate site into a place bursting with life to the thread of promise that was woven throughout the process they had lived through since their arrival in Yemin Orde. No less, from the vantage point of adulthood, our graduates remembered the womb-like spaces in which their dreams had been kindled.

Instead of fearing and thus negating the teenage urge to group together in places of refuge from the all-seeing eye of the adults, we subtly suggested to our teenagers the *Jonah's whale* option. Because, again, the warmth and intimacy of teenage bonding can bear seeds resulting in the unexpected excitement and fulfillment of true accomplishment.

Time and time again, as I have followed the stories of our graduates who have transformed collapsed psyches into wombs gestating new life for themselves and their society, I have learned that these associations and reassurances carry enormous hidden power.

Recently, Alexandra, a graduate of ours who is now the mother of a teenager, asked me what I thought about her discussion with her daughter who was wondering whether to imitate her friends by buying a lock for her door and putting up a "Private. Do Not Enter" sign.

"I don't really need it, Mom," her daughter had told her. This stunned Alexandra, because as a teenager growing up in our Village, she had always dreamed of a completely private room.

"Is it normal," she asked me, "that my own daughter seems to have less of a need for privacy than her friends?"

My response was, "You apparently radiated to your

daughter that her privacy is the fulfillment of your dreams. Maybe that is why she doesn't need a lock and sign to keep you out of her domain."

Mediating the World

In Yemin Orde, the world is constantly, almost every day, penetrating and interacting with the world of our youth. As these lines are written, Yemin Orde is hosting refugee children from Guinea Bissau, who saw their parents slaughtered in ethnic warfare and made it across the continent of Africa to the Israeli border. Arrested for crossing illegally into the country, Yemin Orde told the police we would take responsibility for these children. One of the rewards for us is that the teens at Yemin Orde have the opportunity to hear, and respond to, these children's story. The sense of identification and involvement in the fate of these children broadens the horizons of our adolescents' life.

It is important to us that the commercial media not be the exclusive mediator of the stories of suffering and survival coming to us from the big world outside. The media is a source of information, but it is as a community that we explore and interpret the information, as if at a village council. Family meetings in which issues are discussed and the possibility of action explored are a critical tool nowadays for providing the sense of permeability and life within the stability of the family circle that teenagers need. While the computer and television are certainly legitimate sources of information, too often today they are considered private domains, with each member of the family "consuming" the news from the outside world individually. Instead, the information brought by the news media, like a messenger arriving in a village from places close or far, should be discussed and digested within the intimate public space that defines the familial connection. This is part of the translation we need to make, in which the urban family adopts and adapts key elements of the lost village.

Institutions, like some families, have a tendency to organize themselves, consciously or unconsciously, in a way that provides for their own survival over time. This means that institutions, for the most part, prefer predictability to surprise and control to flexibility. Especially in residential education campuses, in which a child lives and learns 24/ 7, the institutional drive towards predictability and control runs counter to the teenager's need to feel the flow of life. Teenagers need to be part of a living community, organized around the life of its members, not an abstract institution whose basic commitment is to its own self-preservation. To the extent that teenagers feel that the place they are living is devoid of an authentic pulse of life, but instead geared towards moving its charges through a set of predetermined hoops, they will experience institutional life as prison. In one way or another they will try to escape, either inwardly, through emotional withdrawal, or outwardly, in emphatic rebellion.

An Unmovable Platform

The biggest existential problem for teenagers – one that by nature is nearly insurmountable – is that they have not yet made it in the world. Although a teenager's self-conception is often "I am who I might become," they can also sense that thus far their dreams are still only fantasies. Especially where teenagers have no real experience in taking responsibility within a family, the future can seem like a black hole. We have taken note of this in regards to children of immigrants and refugees who have had to negotiate the narrow bridge into a new culture, where the familiar codes and survival strategies no longer apply. For these children, whose parents' lives usually do not fit into our media-influenced and materialistic models of success, trying to envision the future is like peering into an impenetrable mist.

Our observations lead us to believe that even children from middle class or wealthy homes with parents who are members of the mainstream of society feel insecure about their future. In fact, these adolescents may feel that they have grown up so cushioned from reality that they have little confidence in their own abilities in spite of the positive reinforcement they may have received from parents and teachers. As noted before, adolescents' source of knowledge of the future comes from the screens and soundtracks of the virtual world. Moreover, this post-modern hyper-technological world is changing at such an accelerated pace that no parent can give their child a completely solid sense of the future.

Within that cloud of uncertainty teenagers need to find an unmovable platform, a place beyond the shifting sands from which they can mount their forays into the world. Adolescence is a journey, yet there has to be a place for every teenager where he or she feels that they have already "made it," already arrived.

Every year, a group of more than 20 teens from the slums of Rio de Janeiro and Sao Paulo join our Village. Some come from neighborhoods of tin roofed shacks with no running water, and streams of sewage flowing in the streets; places where the mortality rate for children is heartbreakingly high, and where the lives of adults are often tragically cut short.

When these Brazilian youngsters first arrive in Yemin Orde they are taken on a tour of the campus. In the office they can see the aerial photo of the entire Village that is mounted on the wall.

"You see this?" I tell them, showing them the borders of the Village, demarcated by a dirt fire road that can be seen clearly on the map. "Every stone of every building, every leaf on every tree, has been waiting for you to arrive."

I want each child to feel that this place is theirs, that they are connected not just to the buildings and the trees, but also to the earth beneath the floor tiles. The ability of even children who have suffered terrible losses and negligence to connect and internalize such a message strikes me over and over again as miraculous. It took me many years of seeing this happen to realize how remarkable are the adolescent powers for renewal and healing.

There are a number of messages I am trying to convey to the youngsters as I introduce them to Yemin Orde. I want them to know that their existence at Yemin Orde is not contingent. I want them to know that in our Village living comes first and learning second. This principle is built into the architecture of our Village. Whereas in many boarding situations children are housed within the same complex that also contains the classrooms and laboratories, at Yemin Orde we are careful to separate the residential area, which represents living, from the school, which represents academic achievement. We have wholeheartedly endorsed this separation despite the distinct and sometimes even contemptuous negative reactions of bureaucratic and academic echelons, who are rigidly locked into their surety that formal education should dominate all else in the children's lives.

The walk between home, on the western slope of the Village, and the school in its east, takes more than a few minutes, and one area cannot be seen from the other. We want our children to understand clearly that success or failure at school will not affect their membership in the Yemin Orde community. This policy is based on the conviction that in the long run the distinct separation between home and school, when it does not supplant the message that performing well at school, is still important to us, actually helps academic excellence. In no way should we allow home to be perceived as merely a branch of school.

The delicate balance between encouraging and helping our children academically, while underlining the separation between school and home, leads to better results in terms of producing youth with a capacity and enthusiasm for learning.

Teenagers need to feel this message from parents as well, not verbally, but emotionally. Just as our Village separates the children's homes from the school, parents need to separate within their own minds their expectations regarding their teenager's performance and behavior from their unconditional and unshakable commitment and bond. If, as parents, we can do that within our own minds, our adolescent children will feel it in our words and deeds as well.

Even within the context of parental involvement in schools, which as we all know is of crucial importance, we have to be careful to keep this awareness in mind. As much as this is highly desirable, we must stand vigilant in order to prevent the culture of even the best schools from penetrating the home. Otherwise, there is a danger that home will no longer be home. Parents should function as the extended self of the child, must encircle their child emotionally and must not be perceived as automatic allies of the school. This, of course, does not mean that teachers' remarks, concerns and advice should in any way be discounted. But adolescents should always feel free to talk about their teachers and school experiences at home without a sense of threat emanating from a suspicion that their parents sympathy is with the other side.

With regard to our visiting Brazilian teenagers, in causing them to think and feel that the entire Village has been conceived and built "just for them," we intend to compensate them for the negligence and abandonment that they have previously experienced – for the years in which they have not been at the center of anybody's life. We are also conveying that, despite their transitory character, the teenage years are foundational. That no matter how deeply they have been wounded in childhood, adolescence still provides the opportunity to heal.

The map of Yemin Orde is a metaphor for what, as parents and educators, we need to strive to give to our teenagers, namely a world that is both bounded and whole. Bounded because the opposite, abandonment, is borderless; the dread of infinite drifting. There needs to be an element of isolation in order to provide the contours of a home. That is why we are insistent on separating home and school. Teens need an environment in which their fragmented psyche, stretched between past and future, childhood and maturity, can find a depiction of wholeness. They need boundaries in order to provide them with at least a provisional sense of solidity, a platform, as we have said, where they can safely stand and assemble the fragments of their life into a unified whole.

Messianic Eyes to See What Is Real

But wholeness cannot be created by boundaries alone. In telling the Brazilian youngsters that everything in Yemin Orde has been waiting for them, I am telling them that this wholeness belongs to them because it reflects a wholeness that they already carry within themselves. The presence of a significant adult figure able to see the potential wholeness that exists in a teenager already, who can see beyond their current fragmented identity, is crucial. In many cultures, eyes are understood to be more than passive receptacles of sight, but to have a deeper power that emanates from them, that can bring blessing or cause damage, depending on the intent of the seer.

In Jewish folklore some of the righteous are said to have "Messianic eyes," meaning they can see how others would look in a redeemed world, when their best potential has been realized. We have to train ourselves to look at our adolescents with this kind of eyes. Without the transforming presence of adults who are able to give these youngsters a sense that they are responding to them not only as they are now, but also as they someday will be, boundaries might quickly become a prison from which they would push to escape. Only the living presence of an adult "guide" who sees the teenager through the prism of an inner roadmap can create a world that is both secure and dynamic enough to allow the adolescent journey of exploration to continue.

We constantly need to remind ourselves that in previous generations the path to adulthood was more or less clearly defined. Firm models existed that provided distinct goals around which teenagers could form their identity. The gentleman, the farmer, the nobleman, the warrior, the scholar and the priest were all archetypes towards which a well-trodden path already led. It's true that often the choices an adolescent faced were constricting in the extreme. The son of serfs could not grow up to be a nobleman. Class structures were very rigid. And for women, in particular, the kind of roles towards which they could aspire was even more limited, no matter what class they came from.

And yet we do not need to idealize the past in order to be fully aware of the problematic nature of the present. Today's world is filled with so much uncertainty that few of us can guarantee our children's long-term future. What we can do is to ensure our adolescents that they have a firm platform to stand on, and that this platform will eventually connect them to the next stage in life, the next platform.

Here in Yemin Orde we have tried to take advantage of our ability to shape the environment in order to create a world that reflects the totality of our youths' concerns; that addresses their depth dimension as well as their physical or intellectual needs. Not every parent or educator can shape the environment in the way we do here. Yet an adult who plays a significant role in a teenager's life can help provide a virtual platform, a place where an adolescent can feel secure and relax into living, because all of him or her is being seen. It is only by relating to many dimensions of a child's life that we can help catalyze inner change in our relationship with our teenagers. This kind of change will allow the adolescent to locate their strengths and compensate for their weaknesses, to gather and use all the powers that life has placed under their command.

Chapter Seven
Adolescent Quest for Justice

Fighting for a Home

The Padani family lived in little more than a shack on the outskirts of Southern Tel Aviv. The mother and father had arrived in Israel from an Islamic country in the Middle East with neither means nor education. They only had each other. The nearly ruined apartment they found soon after reaching Israel was part of an abandoned building, and it took all they could to make it into a home. Both worked hard at menial jobs and every year seemed to bring another child, until finally the family numbered 14 children. During one of the frequent attempts of Mr. Padani to expand the living area of the family home, an iron support bar fell on his leg, permanently crippling him.

Now unable to fend for their children, the Padanis became dependent on welfare. The younger children were taken away from their home, which was considered potentially in danger of physical collapse. Three of the teenagers were placed in our Village. Angry over having been forced to leave home, the three young sons refused to cooperate and lashed out against our counselors and the other youngsters. All the attempts we made to bring them into the life of the Village and integrate them into daily activities failed. The date that the Tel Aviv municipality had set for the destruction of their childhood home approached and overshadowed all our attempts to channel them towards new endeavors.

At the basis of the Yemin Orde community lies the axiom that an individual's plight is the plight of all of us. In this case in particular, the Padani brothers' crisis resonated with our youngsters – the concrete threat that their family home would be razed served as a potent metaphor for the destruction of home that most of our youth had experienced one way or another.

With our encouragement the day of the proposed house razing became a central focus for the Village youngsters. The case had reached the newspapers, and our teens, even those who rarely read unless they had to, hungrily devoured and compared the different accounts. They learned that the Padanis, despite their poverty, were a loving and unified family. They sensed, also, that a home needs to rest on the preparations and prior achievements of the parents, which alone can guarantee it solid foundations.

The kids sought out knowledge of the legalities governing house destruction and whether the situation might possibly be reversed. As the date of the bulldozers approached the whole Village felt, mentally and emotionally, that they had become the "House of Padani." It was also clear, without our having to say so, that if the Padanis were left homeless, Yemin Order Youth Village would be their home for the time being.

When the day came, the Padani brothers arrived, accompanied by four busloads of their newly extended family, to protect their home. When remembering those hours, I still ask myself whether it was indeed responsible to an educator like me to go ahead with the children's quest to realize their sense of justice by opposing the ruling of the court. I knew, though, that we had to be faithful to our guiding principle regarding the purity and power of the adolescent quest for justice, which we see as an outburst from the depth of their humanity, and not merely a developmental stage categorized by theory or another. There is no way to escape with the help of words in situations where only deeds can reaffirm such basic beliefs and conceptions.

Needless to say, we ensured our youngsters' safety in the face of the bulldozers and police, though our hearts occasionally skipped a beat out of concern that the real life drama could veer out of control. Fortunately, the youths' efforts led to a delay in the house-razing, which gave the welfare authorities time to engage in a search for a decent alternative housing solution, eventually finding the apartment where the parents live today. After this experience, the Padani brothers' attitude toward the Village totally changed, and the Village collectively felt a deep sense of achievement.

The Passion for Justice as a Pure Flame

This anecdote from the life of our Village is one of the more extreme manifestations of the power of the teenage pursuit for justice. Yet, on the whole, teenagers' passion for justice is no weaker than their drive for excitement and adventure. Youth movements are able to channel this energy into campaigns that help the character of adolescents, while catalyzing social change.

Israel itself – its *kibbutz* movement and its defense force – was built through the power of young people's desire to create a new world based on the pillars of justice.

Infants are born to their mothers and the circle of their immediate family, but the meaning of teenage rebirth is to be born again within the circle of society. The teenage attempt to forge an identity, to find a place for themselves within their peer group and beyond, in society at large, is part of a process akin to an infant's efforts to learn to crawl, walk and talk. The teenager must eventually break out beyond the family to forge a link with a mentor, and together to create a new unit that will be recognized within the larger framework of society.

As we know, a toddler learning to talk experiences

the plasticity of language, playing with sounds and meanings as adults only rarely do. The process of acquiring language for the first time brings children back to the very roots and origins of language. Perhaps this is why young children have the capacity to learn several languages at once. Similarly, for adolescents, the necessity of finding a place within a society of peers, forging an identity and eventually choosing a direction within society at large brings them back to the roots of society, and thus to what could be defined as a natural obsession with justice. The question of justice, of the way things *should* be, is at the heart of the matter when we are dealing with the basic material of society's formation.

If an adult's sense of identity is centered around that part of the self that has been actualized, the teenager's identity is connected more directly with a sense of their own potential: "I am who I can imagine myself to be."

Questions of justice, of the fairness of life and society are intimately related to teenagers' ability to imagine their potential realized. In an unjust society a particular individual's possibilities for fulfillment are often blocked by a power structure that favors those with entrenched privileges, while in a perfectly just society every teenager will ultimately receive the chance to realize their self and their talents.

Instead, if we perceive the teenager's concern with justice as a pure and unadulterated flame rising spontaneously from within, we may feel this flame rekindled within ourselves. The linguist, Noam Chomsky, theorized that children have an innate ability to learn language; that what he termed the "deep structure" of grammar and syntax are built into the human brain, waiting to be activated. When working with teenagers, it often seems as if the desire to see justice done – within the family, society and in the world – is built into the structure of the human soul, and bursts out passionately during the course of adolescence.

Despite its potentially volatile nature, the adolescent obsession with justice should be seen as a gift of inestimable value by parents and educators. Part of our goal in raising adolescents should be to recognize, preserve and develop their craving for justice and their wish to make the world a better place. This aspiration is already actually present in an intrinsic fashion. What hope does the world have if this characteristic, instead of being cherished and encouraged, is allowed to wither, or worse yet, is treated with disdain? When the burning passion for justice with which young people are endowed is repeatedly dampened or extinguished, cynicism often takes its place.

This flame of passion for justice – *Tikkun Olam* – that burns within our teenagers' souls deserves our attention, protection and active guidance.

Chapter Eight

Tikkun HaLev

Education Emanating from Body and Soul

Psychological language is inappropriate for parents and educators who must meet their teenager children as-is, in the midst of life. Our emphasis is not in seeing the pathological, abnormal side of adolescence. It is a normality we want to focus on. Hasn't the time arrived for us to reassess and broaden our notion of what is normal?

Along with psychological language, we must distance ourselves from a technocratic approach to child-rearing which weakens the natural flow of relationship between parents or educators and children. Instead, we need to feel our power to educate, to mediate life to others, as something located within our own bodies and souls.

To this end we have developed over the years a symbolic and conceptual language consisting of two lines-one horizontal and one vertical – and two concentric circles that define the shape, reach, and direction of human existence. The horizontal line stretches between past and future, while the vertical line rises from the center of the circle – from the existential present that we call the earth point – towards the heavens, towards transcendent values and faith. The inner circle represents our awareness of self, and the continuing spiraling effort to achieve growth and insight, while the outer circle represents the outer boundaries of the world that effects us and that we can effect-the social world that surrounds us. We call these two circles the circle of *Tikkun Halev* or mending of the heart, and *Tikkun Olam*, the mending of the world. The concept of *Tikkun* is central to the Jewish notion that human beings

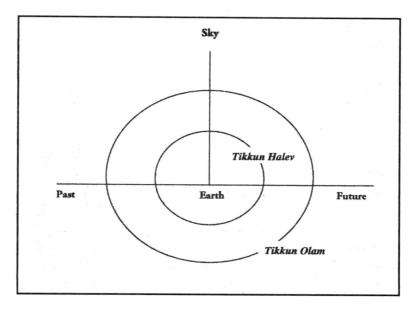

are partners with God. God left creation in an imperfect state in order to allow us to play a role in transforming the world and making it whole.

The lines and circles simultaneously direct us inwards, helping us locate our own center of gravity, and outwards, enabling us to see our teenagers in a multi-dimensional fashion. The lines and circles create a symbolic structure that serves to make vivid for us the basic parameters of our own world and the adolescent's. We then have a better chance of perceiving him in a holistic fashion. It is a mnemonic device to remind me how to fill my relationship with my teenage child with emotional content, so that I am not perceived as absent or as one-dimensional.

At the same time, these very same lines and circles remind us that what we are seeing of our teenagers at anyone moment is always only partial. The line that represents time cuts through the center of the circles, dividing them into two halves. The bottom half of the circle is like the dark side of the moon, present, but invisible. We are always only partly revealed, even to ourselves, certainly to others. The half circle below the line running from past to future represents the depth dimension, the place where experiences, wounds and secret hopes are stored. Keeping just this one idea in mind as we face our teenagers will already transform our relationship with them.

The center point of the circles, where the horizontal and vertical lines meet, is the time of our psychological present in which we interact with our children and in which we experience reality. The present is the most fluid of the elements, because it is constantly in formation, and is subject to all the stimuli and variables of the ever-changing kaleidoscope we call life. The other elements, which we keep touching and reinforcing, are anchors that serve to affix a sense of stability to the present moment.

Earth represents the actual reality, the environment, emotional surroundings and conditions of the adolescent's existential present. It is, so to speak, that which is closest to him, the ground below his feet. And we must pay attention to this ground. With all their defiant desire for independence, teenagers still want to be mothered. They want us to notice if they are hungry, cold or tired, if their room is a mess, if they need immediate physical or emotional help. Through our gentle, non-intrusive attention to their "Earth" dimension, we can demonstrate our embrace of them. Being aware of the earth point means also being aware of one's own current situation.

Try not to allow yourself to be swept away from your parental task of awareness by shifting moods or needs. When facing your child, the flashing thought of the lines and the circles can be like igniting the flame of a match in order to illuminate a dark cavern.

The vertical line points from earth upwards, towards the transcendent, towards the ideas and ideals that guide our lives. An idealistic drive is one of the primary characteristics of adolescents, and if we are to be part of their world, we need to recognize this. Part of what we have to do as parents or educators is to clarify the ideals that are important to us. Our ideals may have faded, raising teenagers' challenges us to shine them up.

These are the four elements, then, that define our two lines: one running from past to future, the second rising from earth towards the sky. The past, both the adolescent's own past, his childhood and all that that entails, and his collective past, the past of his family and his culture. The future: his own future, which is already alive in his imagination and his heart as his destination and the source of his future identity as well as the future of the world in which he will live. The earth, the ground on which he stands, everything that makes up his day-to-day physical and emotional environment. And the sky, the ideals that fire his ethical imagination, the ideas that help him understand his place in the larger scheme of things.

The two circles – one of which represents the inner realm of the individual human heart, while the other indicates our reaching out to the widening circle of mankind – are representations of wholeness and of the unending process of attempting to reach that wholeness. The circles create boundaries – they represent the impossibility of reaching the unbounded whole, the complete, for who can completely heal themselves or the world?

But the circle, which mathematicians call the perfect form, also means that the part that you are doing has a quality of completeness. We are always dealing with the world of brokeness, but our very willingness to face and touch and try to heal this brokeness in ourselves and others is in itself whole.

The moment that a parent or educator realizes that within the inner world of his or her child there are uncharted depths, things that are hidden from you and also from her, you have touched wholeness. Adolescents, as they search to define their identity, struggle with many kinds of duality that seem to have a life of their own within their questioning consciousness. Am I strong or weak? Good or bad?

Parents must learn to recognize the presence of duality, and understand that each pair of opposites is joined at the root of their teenager's consciousness, like the two sides of a coin. The circle of *Tikkun Halev* advises us that the journey to adulthood is a journey towards integration and healing, in which dualities synergetically integrate into a greater whole.

Every new year in training and retraining our staff, we aspire to introduce utmost clarity into the process of identifying the basic structure of the world that we have to convey to our children if they are to feel secure in their journey. The physical embrace that is a natural part of our response to children can be transformed through a language of symbols and graphic expressions into a way of relating to the world of the adolescent that is a practical translation of Buber's concept of "encirclement" – the existential dimension of the circles of *Tikkun Olam* and *Tikkun HaLev*. Together with the two lines – one running horizontally between past and future, the other vertically from earth to sky – we create the inner map from which we can radiate wholeness.

As a new year begins the trick is to make the images real, so real that you can feel them in your body.

"Stand up and stretch out your arms," I say to a group of young counselors, wishing to transmit the language and images that can activate the potency and applicability that theoretical knowledge lacks. I wish them to feel their power to educate, to mediate life to others, as located within themselves, physically and mentally. In this attempt I have discovered for myself the principle expounded in George B. Leonard's book, *Education and Ecstasy,* namely, that all true educational paths have a foundation in ecstatic experience.

"Imagine that your left arm is stretched out so far that it is touching the past, so that its metaphoric weight is resting on your palm, as if your source is all there: ancestors, culture, memories," I say to them.

"Now turn your head and watch your other arm until your eyes reach your palm, where the metaphoric weight of your future rests. Close your eyes, and feel time flowing from one outstretched palm to the other, the past moving through you towards the future. Feel the weight of your presence, your center. Slowly pull the past and the future towards yourself, towards the center. Feel how solidly your feet are standing on the earth, feel your full presence. Now lift your attention upwards, towards the sky, towards the infinite. Let your inner voice remind you of your highest aspirations and beliefs."

After reviewing numerous educational or psychological theories, it is important to me that our staff feel that education emanates primarily from our specificity and our depth – from body and soul, from our center of gravity. This is, after all, what each of our adolescents is seeking in us.

To ultimately hone this inner sense of our sharpened relevance in our children's world, we move to the next step: Feeling how the lines that define our being are set within the two concentric circles.

"Turn around one full revolution," I suggest. "Feel the limits of your being. Imagine two concentric circles defining this limit. Sense the circle closest to yourself, immediately surrounding you, defining and enclosing your existential experience. Now imagine the circle farthest away, the outer boundary of where your awareness reaches. Can you feel these circles defining for you a platform within the infinite? Can they also represent the space into which each of us can grow?"

When we find our center of gravity within these two circles, the circle of *Tikkun HaLev* and the circle of *Tikkun Olam,* our sense of presence is activated. We radiate the inner parental quality of genuine wholeness. This priceless moment of insight is the cornerstone of our transformation as significant parental mentors.

Over the years I have become convinced that this exercise, and the conceptual world that informs it, have helped us find the archetypal village that defines human hopes and enabled us to infuse the Yemin Orde Village with its almost utopian quality. This has made our Village a place in which both staff and teenagers can cope with tensions, outbursts and differences of opinion without needing to shatter and shock. This simple exercise, absorbed and internalized, can charge the air in which the relationship between adults and teenagers is transpiring with positive electrolytes, by serving as a basic outline onto which the contents of our experience in life can affix itself. It is a mnemonic device that reminds me how to fill my relationship with my teenage child with emotional content, so that I am not perceived as absent or as one-dimensional.

Earth and Sky, Past and Future

The center point of our two circles, where the horizontal and vertical lines meet, is the time of our psychological present; the very particular moment in which we interact with our children and in which we experience reality. This center point is the immediate environment, the current space-time coordinate in which our teenage child and we are alive. The present is the most fluid of the elements, because it is constantly in formation and is subject to all the stimuli and variables of the ever-changing kaleidoscope we call life, from the weather to the current emotional and physical state of each person. In fact, because existential time, the time of the present, is so fluid, and because we have so little control of what is going to happen to us at every particular moment, we arrange the elements in our consciousness so that the present is constantly in the center, whatever we are doing. The other elements, which we keep touching and reinforcing, are anchors that serve to affix a sense of stability to the present moment. Touching these elements can provide for our children a meaningful and reassuring context. They also remind us of the total situation of their life so that we are not harmfully distracted by the emotions and attitudes they throw in our face at any given moment.

Representing movement from the past, from where we have already been, towards the future, where we are going, the horizontal line thus marks the principal vector of the adolescent's journey, which like our own, is a journey through time. The vertical line begins in the existential present, at the center between past and future – "earth" – and it extends upwards towards a transcendent horizon that is beyond time – "sky." "Earth" represents the actual reality; the environment, emotional surroundings, and conditions of adolescents' existential present. It is, so to speak, that which is closest to them, the ground below their feet.

And we must pay attention to this ground. With all their defiant desire for independence, teenagers still want to be mothered. They want us to notice if they are hungry, cold or tired, if their room is a mess, or if they need immediate physical or emotional help. Through our gentle, non-intrusive attention to their "earth" dimension, we can demonstrate our embrace of them. Parents are often concerned that if they respond too generously to their children's constant demands, they will "spoil" them. And certainly, teenagers should be encouraged to take a large share of responsibility in tending to their own needs and pitching in on household chores. But what parents call "spoiling," an overdeveloped anxiety about one's immediate environment and an inability to delay gratification, is usually learned from the parents themselves. Since children internalize and embody our attitude towards them, when we are able to wholeheartedly gesture our love and care by responding to our children's needs, we are likely to be rewarded with goodhearted children who are attentive to the needs of others.

To be aware of the earth element, which is the center point of our diagram, means to focus in on the details of the particular moment. What are the pressures, both physical and psychological, that are affecting your adolescent at this particular moment in their life?

Being aware of the earth point means also being aware of one's own current situation. Are you tired, aloof, disappointed, angry or even hungry? How is your physical or emotional state affecting your responses to your child? Notice this and adjust accordingly. Or, at the very least, don't blame your children for what is going on inside of you. Try not to allow yourself to be swept away from your parental task of awareness by your shifting moods or needs. While it may seem inconceivable to take all of what is going on within yourself into account in real time when facing your child, the flashing symbol of the lines and the circles can be like igniting a flame in order to illuminate a dark cavern.

The vertical line points from earth upwards, towards the transcendent – towards the ideas and ideals that guide our lives. They may be guiding ideals such as justice, peace or love of humanity, or they me be love of God and obedience to religious teachings. Whatever their form, ideals will always be an important component of a wholesome life. An idealistic drive is one of the primary characteristics of adolescents, and if we are to be part of their world, we need to recognize this. Part of what we have to do as parents or educators is to clarify the ideals that are important to us. Our ideals may have faded; raising teens challenges us to polish them up.

By presenting our ideals to our teenagers – not in the form of a fiat, but in a way that will nourish teenage idealism – we can help them express their own idealistic drive. Teenagers will often reject the ideals we share with them. For many teenagers this is almost necessary if they are eventually to embrace them as their own. This should not faze us. Ultimately, years later, our children may surprise us by returning to the values they once decisively rejected. Our job is not to lock teenagers into specific ideals, but rather to show them a universe in which ideals matter.

These are the four elements, then, that define our two lines: one running from past to future, the second rising from earth towards the sky. The past, again, is adolescents' own past, their childhood and all that that entails, and their collective past, the past of their family and culture. The future is both their own future, which is already alive in their imagination and heart as the destination and the source of their future identity, and the future of the world in which they will live. The earth is the ground on which they stand, everything that makes up his day-to-day physical and emotional environment. And the sky is the ideals that fire their ethical imagination, and the ideas that help them understand their place in the larger scheme of things.

The moment that you as a parent or educator realizes that within the inner world of your child there are uncharted depths, things that are hidden from you and also from him or her, you have touched wholeness. Adolescents, as they search to define their identity, struggle with many dualities that seem to have a life of their own within their questioning consciousness. Am I strong or weak? Good or bad? Attractive or repulsive? A success or a failure? Parents must learn to recognize the presence of duality, and understand that each pair of opposites is joined at the root of their teenager's consciousness, like the two sides of a coin.

Too often, parents are locked into either a hypercritical mode or a discourse that allows mostly for sweet praise and positive reinforcement. While it is easy to understand the destructive nature of constant criticism, merely giving positive reinforcement without being aware of the other side of the coin will also ultimately boomerang, building up children's suspicions of a lack of authenticity and ultimately polluting the dialogue and interaction between adults and children.

The circle of *Tikkun HaLev* is all about balancing between dualities, helping us to recognize the wholeness they in fact create within our child and within us. It also helps us to recognize the subconscious depths that lie below the level of immediate, existential awareness. These are also part of the adolescent mind, as they are part of our own psyche. Our awareness of the circle of *Tikkun HaLev* advises us that the journey to adulthood is a journey towards integration and healing, in which dualities synergistically integrate into a greater whole.

Spirals of Insight and Transformation

The circle of *Tikkun HaLev* represents insight; the ability to learn from the suffering we have endured and the mistakes we have made through inner reflection. Why a circle? Because insight is produced when a new experience touches an old one - a memory, wound or a blind spot – and we suddenly understand, and are illuminated. The seemingly unrelenting forward movement of our existence in time, represented by the horizontal line stretching from past to future, actually loops back upon itself when we gain insight. Later events, through their parallels and similarities, shed light on earlier ones. Our experiences as we move through the straight line of time can seem arbitrary; when time becomes a circle, we see the contours of a story, of our story. The circle thus surrounds and protects us by allowing us to feel that life has meaning.

The flow of the year through the seasons is another way in which the circular aspect of time is revealed. Religious and secular holidays are marked at exactly the same point every year, and every week in Yemin Orde, as in other Jewish communities, a section of the Torah is read and discussed. In this fashion the Five Books of Moses are completed every year. On *Simchat Torah*, the last day of the fall festival of *Succot,* the last words of the Torah are read and immediately Genesis is begun again. Commentators throughout the generations have noted that when the last letter of the Torah is connected to the first letter of the Torah, the letters spell *Lev,* or "heart." The heart gains knowledge as we allow the same teachings to touch and penetrate the new experiences we have celebrated or suffered during the year. The linear course of time is thus encircled with insight.

"Torapy" — Bedtime Stories for the Wounded Heart

The disturbing aspects of day-to-day life hit adolescents with a primal force to which adults have largely become inured. One vital insight that all great literary traditions can impart upon teenagers is that they are not alone in their agonizing quandaries. The dualistic structure of adolescent thought means that teens tend to split reality into categories of good and evil, purity and defilement; when these categories collapse, the conclusions they draw are often harsh and disturbing. When a teenager witnesses disharmony in the family, unfaithfulness or dishonesty, or when he or she is disappointed by a trusted someone or his or herself, he or she often experiences overwhelming feelings of broken-ness and heartbreak. The world seems dark and their existential state is one of inconsolable grief. Teenage despair is heightened by a sense of being utterly alone in their knowledge and situation, as if they were unique in perceiving the falseness and tragedy that permeate the world.

Bedtime stories ease the fears of young children as they travel towards the unknown of night and sleep. They renew children's emotional connection with their parents even as they provide the children with a language that articulates and interprets their fears. During the teenage years great works of literature can play the role that bedtime stories did during early childhood – addressing unspoken fears and strengthening intergenerational connections. Especially when mediated by adult mentors, stories from the great literary traditions can ease the sting of this loneliness, transforming what teenagers thought they were carrying in solitude into part of the human condition, and thus opening up a space for dialogue and integration.

In our Village I use the Book of Books, the Torah, whose pedigree of ancientness and sacredness is for us unsurpassed. Half jokingly, I call the weekly themes with which I flood the Village consciousness, "Torapy," Torah messages that are aimed at the wounded, growing heart.

As often as possible I will try to touch on the primal conflicts, contradictions and dilemmas so prevalent in the biblical narrative: brother killing brother, drunkenness as an escape and humiliation, fathers sacrificing sons, sexual misadventures, jealousy between sisters and so on. By being as sharp, even as outrageous as possible, I hope to bring to the surface adolescent obsessions whose repression drains psychic energy.

"King David took a married woman!" I might

exclaim, hoping to open the closed subject of marital betrayals and ruined families that many children in our Village and elsewhere carry as a secret burden. I might shout, in our weekly discussion, "How could a father sell his son?" in reference to Reuben's promise to his father, Jacob, knowing full well that many of the children in the Village feel, by varying degrees, that they have been abandoned by their parents. By linking such painful themes to the narrative of the Torah, I convey to them a broader context of sanctity and wholesomeness. By emphasizing the way in which even the greatest of biblical heroes struggled with potentially devastating flaws and temptations, I hope to ameliorate the paralyzing effect weakness and corruption often have on teenage minds.

Through "Torapy" we ultimately wish to convey the message that brokenness and wholeness can coexist in our world, and that the dualities that haunt teenagers bear the possibility of integration. For example, in Genesis, God instructs Abraham to seal their covenant by splitting the bodies of three sacrificial animals and walking between them, while leaving the body of a sacrificial bird whole. I tease out the symbolism of this story, emphasizing the bird left whole as the ultimate vision of wholeness and unification whose imprint remains before us even as we journey through an often broken and fragmented reality.

The phrase ". . .and the bird was not divided" is repeated over and over again during the week of its Torah portion, posted on the bulletin board and mentioned on our community television broadcasts, until it is lodged in the memory of the teens to take with them through life. Whenever they recall that phrase, they will recall a cluster of associations about broken-ness and wholeness, reality and radical hope.

My hope is that our children take at least one provocative phrase from each of the fifty-odd weekly Torah portions with them on their journey through life. This cycle of ideas and phrases are like doors through which they can enter a system that has its own inner logic and wholeness. I sometimes call these phrases *mantras*, because our intention is that, through repetition, they become absorbed into the subconscious, emerging into the conscious mind when necessary. In a sense, though, they are the opposite of mantras. Instead of a hypnotic, meditative effect, these phrases should catalyze critical thinking, to remind our youngsters of the larger frameworks of life beyond their immediate situation and to locate them within the intergenerational web across which living wisdom is transmitted.

On at least one occasion one of our graduates has told me how a "Torapy" phrase literally saved two lives. Fassil, an Ethiopian youngster, had the bad luck of falling under the command of an abusive officer during basic military training. This officer was apparently threatened by Fassil's blackness. In any event he took advantage of every occasion to remind Fassil that he was "primitive" and racially and culturally different.

"When he shamed me in front of my whole platoon, I could feel the blood rushing to my head. I felt myself losing control, about to turn my automatic rifle on him, I was so furious. Then I remembered what you had taught us, *Tal beidna Sagidle*." It is a quotation from the Talmud that explains why Jacob bowed before his own son, Joseph, meaning "the fox will speak in its time," or every dog has his day.

Fassil said, "I was suddenly able to look at my officer as a dog having his day. And I knew that I would have my day as well. I felt my hand, which had begun to tighten around my weapon, relax."

On another occasion, in a phone call out of the blue from another army officer, who sounded puzzled and bemused, I heard the following story: "Shai, who I understand is one of your former charges, is on trial at our base for disobedience. I'm his judge. He told me that if I want to understand him, I should call you and say the code words 'Vayigash Eilav Yehuda'."

I knew immediately what Shai meant. Those three words, which mean "And Judah approached him," describe Judah's lion-hearted decision to confront the Egyptian viceroy who has arrested his brother, Benjamin. Judah still does not know that the viceroy is actually his long lost brother, Joseph. Because of this scene, conveyed by these three words, Judah has become our symbol of the moral power of the individual confronting authority with courage.

What had happened was that Shai had been assigned kitchen duty, and had seen how the army kitchen threw out enormous quantities of bread each day. In our Village we had always preached that throwing away bread when there are hungry people in the world is a sin. Shai had gone on strike, refusing to take part in training until the army found a way to get the bread to those who needed it. "You have a Judah on your hands," I told his officer.

Fixing Your All

The psychological healing that accompanies a successful journey from adolescence to adulthood cannot take place in isolation. Through "Torapy," we connect *Tikkun HaLev* with an ancient tradition whose major focus is the transformation of the world. This is the outer circle of *Tikkun Olam*. A central component of Yemin Orde's message is that we are all part of something larger than ourselves, part of a human community that needs us just as we need it. Our self-definition and our healing is part of a process leading towards *Tikkun Olam*, the fixing of the world. In Jewish philosophy the trajectory of human history is leading towards a messianic time, envisioned by the prophets, in which violence and corruption will cease, and knowledge, peace and brotherhood will fill the earth.

Gershom Scholem, one of the preeminent academic scholars of Judaism of the 20th century and a friend and contemporary of Martin Buber, pointed out that the Jewish concept of Messianic redemption differs from the Christian concept in at least one important way. For Christians, who believe that the messiah has already come, a person can experience messianic redemption through their relationship with Jesus, regardless of the current state of the world. In Jewish tradition messianic redemption means the transformation of the physical, concrete world. Personal redemption cannot be disconnected from the redemption of all of life. There exists a profound relationship between a person's own individual spiritual development and his efforts to "bring the Messiah" – to catalyze the transformation of humanity for which we are all waiting.

A Hassidic master, named the Alexander Rebbe after the Polish town in which he lived, expressed this relationship succinctly. He said that a person is comprised of many different parts, but also has an "all," a totality that is more than the sum of their parts.

It is possible to purify and fix all the different parts of oneself in isolation from others, the Rabbi of Alexander said. But if you want to fix your "all," your wholeness, the totality of yourself, you have to be engaged in bringing the Messiah, in working for *Tikkun Olam*. The two concentric circles represent this relationship, *Tikkun HaLev* widens into *Tikkun Olam*. And the reverse is true as well. Learning to identify and connect with the pain of others is a key part of *Tikkun Olam*, by healing the loneliness that is at the heart of many of our wounds, and is thus a catalyst of *Tikkun HaLev*.

On a simpler level we can understand the relationship between the two *Tikkuns* by returning to our traditional village. Ultimately, the journey to adulthood in a traditional village means a journey to a position of respect and honor within the community. To be a respected adult means to have acquired wisdom of the kind that is used to solve disputes between neighbors, to make peace between man and wife and to negotiate good relations between rival tribes. Human beings are communal by nature, and there is a deep and significant relationship between self-fulfillment and the kind of communal responsibility that we can identify as the drive towards *Tikkun Olam*.

The circle of *Tikkun Olam* binds us together with our children in our shared quest for a better world. It reminds us that the very act of parenting or educating is part of that quest. Parents do not choose their children, and their children are not meant to be young clones who will realize their parent's unfulfilled ambitions or assuage their parent's egos with their accomplishments. Sound parenting means realizing that the responsibility of raising children to a happy, healthy and productive adulthood is part of *Tikkun Olam*. An essential part of the healthy adulthood we are raising them towards is one in which the drive towards *Tikkun Olam* is legitimized and strengthened.

Heights and Depths within Our Teenagers

Relationships with teenagers that are defined by the exercise of one-sided authority are toxic. So is the other extreme; reneging on all hierarchy and the responsibility of guidance. So how can we balance between these two extremes of the pendulum?

Life is a never-ending journey, but in relation to our teenager we must also recognize our role as the person who has, to a certain extent, already arrived. One "proof" of having "arrived," in the eyes of your offspring at least, is that you already have a child to whom you have to show the way. Whether we feel up to it or not, we are role models for our children. The need for adult models is so deep in children and teens that scientists may someday discover that it is genetic. From the materials we give them our children must forge a model of adulthood that they can take with them internally on their journey through life. And in a deeper sense they must learn about themselves and about the world through us, through the universe we forge in our relationship.

Our framework of lines and circles can help us play a significant part in our children's lives without conceiving this role in terms of hierarchy or control, and allow us to conceptualize our children's life as a totality. The symbolic language we use can help us understand that whatever aspect of themselves our teens are revealing at the moment is only a partial expression of who they are – only one part of a duality that they contain within them. This is one of the important insights we have to keep in mind concerning teenagers. They can be one thing one moment, and something completely different the next. Like a deep-sea fisherman, they keep pulling personas out from the depths of their subconscious, trying them out, throwing them back into the waters. We have to show them consistency in our willingness to be patient and loving, without demanding from them a consistency that is just not yet part of who they are.

A River Flowing from Eden

The nature and quality of a parent's intention is something that adolescents instantly absorb. People often under-estimate the ability of children in general and adolescents in particular to interpret non-verbal signals; to understand, in an intuitive but precise way, the emotions that precede and accompany our words.

Jewish mysticism places a great deal of emphasis on the idea of *kol*, or voice, as opposed to *dibbur*, or words.

While the tongue, palate, lips and teeth create the particular sounds of each individual word, the voice emanates from deeper inside of us, from the region of our lungs and heart. Teenagers are sensitive to the source of that emanation. Our voice carries our emotions, like silt being swept downstream from a river's origins, whether we want to reveal how we feel or not. Teens will instantly be able to tell if the voice addressing them is emerging from a heart of stone or crumbling earth – filled with fear, distraction or impatience – or emanating like a living spring from a place of empathy, focus, and concern. Teenagers listen more to certain adults because they reveal something confidence-inspiring or trustworthy from their inner depths when they speak. Their voices are full, rather than hollow.

If we think of every sentence we speak as the lyrics of a song, then the voice is like the melody that colors and carries the words to our hearts. It may happen that a youngster approaches me at a moment in which I am focused on something else. The computer is crashing; I'm late for a meeting, and three key staff members have called in sick. All of us know these situations well. How do I answer this request, which may be presented with great urgency, but to an incidental observer might seem trivial? The split second before I respond is of critical importance. Over-whelmed as I am, the easiest thing would be to answer in a technical fashion, telling the young person quickly and tersely that this is not the right time or that I am not the right person to answer them. But once I have consciously trained myself, until it is second nature, to visualize within myself a reflection of the adolescent's world – a world that includes emotional depths – I can respond in a split second from the depths of my own self, and from there create a line of communication untainted by tension.

In conveying to teenagers that what concerns them also really concerns me, even if I can't deal with it now, my choice of words are not as important as my intonation and the look in my eyes. In the long run teenagers will learn that delay is not rejection, and that credibility need not be measured only in terms of immediate availability. The lines and circles, by helping us focus our attention and our intention, can give us that extra moment of concentration that lifts our response out of the realm of the tense order of daily life. Speaking from the place within us that lies at the center of the circles, where the lines meet, can transform our response from anger, threat and defensiveness into voice and action emanating from an undamaged place within us.

No matter what else is going on in our lives, it is possible to learn to speak from a place of clarity and honesty when in conversation with adolescents. Our voice is like a vector emerging from deep within us. Around that vector a whole world, the world that includes our teenagers and us, crystallizes. The *Zohar*, the central work of the Jewish mystical tradition *Kabbalah*, says that the energy flowing into our world from heaven is like a river of light flowing from the Garden of Eden. Can our voice, emerging from the right place within us, be like the river flowing from Eden?

Along with our voice we should be conscious of our body language when we are with our adolescent children. The way we stand and move and the quality of our touch can subtly shift our relationship with our teenagers to convey strength, grace and warmth. Even when we shake a child's hand, it is possible for our touch linger for a heartbeat longer. Educating is a routine of breaking conventions. When we look into our adolescent's eyes, can we feel assurance pouring from our own eyes towards theirs? Perhaps childhood is so often remembered as a kind of Eden, because people often speak to children from that Eden-like place within themselves, a place of wholeness.

If, without turning our teenagers back into children, we can transmit through our voice, our physical presence and our facial expressions a taste of Eden, we will have accomplished a great deal.

Emotional Channels for Learning

That place of wholeness, the taste of Eden, is of utmost importance for educators as well as parents. Learning itself is often dependent on the kind of emotions educators transmit. I became aware very early on that my intellectual development was affected by the emotional quality that teachers projected. While sitting in the classroom of teachers who radiated some form of parental affection and interest, I was able to absorb even the most difficult material and earn high grades, while the lessons of teachers who were excellent technicians, but emotionally cold, simply did not penetrate into my mind. As a rule, relationship is the medium through which knowledge and cognitive skills can flow from one person to another.

In the *Kabbalah* this is represented by the notion that the light of wisdom can penetrate human minds only when the path is lit by the light of love. The opposite is also true; sarcasm and cynicism on the part of a teacher can close the mind of a student, making it impossible for him or her to learn. One of my high school mathematics teachers once asked me to solve a certain problem he had scrawled on the blackboard.

"I'm not familiar with that kind of problem," I remember telling him. In a tone drenched in sarcasm, the teacher "introduced" me to the problem, "Chaim, meet problem. Problem meet Chaim."
The mocking tone of his voice snapped my mind shut. It took me six months until I was able to begin to absorb mathematics again.

The relationship between learning and emotions is

doubly important when one is dealing with youngsters from uprooted families or families who have been locked into a cycle of social and economic failure. Almost invariably, children from such families who have succeeded in breaking through to a new feeling of competence and confidence have had the benefit of a teacher with whom they felt an emotional, quasi-parental connection. We must never tire of declaring that children's perception, whether conscious or subconscious, of lack of faith in their ability to succeed may very well be the primary cause of poor academic performance among deprived groups.

The emotions, then, are the key with which the process of learning can be unlocked. One of my mentors, Professor Reuven Feurstein, is an educational innovator renowned in Israel and internationally; the main thrust of his work has been to demonstrate the possibility of coaxing out the hidden cognitive abilities of children and teenagers labeled retarded or low achievers. One of his educational axioms is that a child who displays a sample of high-level cognitive ability – a single act, for example, of complex reasoning – carries within him the potential to raise all of his thinking to the same level. But how does Feuerstein elicit this sample? With enormous patience, he may spend hours with a low functioning child, nourishing him or her with loving attention, until evoking the evidence of higher ability that he seeks; a moment that can be a turning point in that child's life.

Sometimes, unlocking the intellect means bringing the learning process unto familiar ground in a teenager's mind, by building on experiences that he or she already knows and trusts. In the case of Tedesse, the young Ethiopian shepherd boy, we asked ourselves how his experience as a shepherd could help him learn the abstract concepts that are of such importance in the Western educational system. The challenge was to go deeper than merely asking him how many sheep would remain in his flock should hyenas stalk and kill three of them. Could his math teacher get him to talk about the many shades of green he remembered in the meadow, or whether the air smelled different when a rainstorm was moving in? To let him describe the whole two weeks he spent alone, or with another friend or two, circling with the sheep through the hills and pastures. Even though these memories might seem to have little to do with mathematics, they may have everything to do with the process of *learning* mathematics, with unclogging the emotional channels through which even mathematics must be absorbed. By bringing memories associated with happiness and competence into the mathematics classroom, as well as by creating an emotional bridge into childhood, the subject matter itself will lose its frightening, alien quality. Tedesse indeed showed a new openness to mathematics once his teacher had internalized the link between emotions and abstract learning.

Sarah: *The Grammar of Nursing*

Sarah was another Ethiopian teen whose experience at Yemin Orde demonstrates the extent to which a child or teen needs an emotional openness or connection to learn. Sarah came to our Village with enormous learning gaps in all the basic school subjects. She was the oldest child in a family of eight and had helped her now divorced mother to raise the other children as she eked out a meager livelihood. Sarah had little psychic energy left over for mastering school. At Yemin Orde she struggled with all of her school subjects, until she had a stroke of luck. Her grammar teacher, Miri, a young woman who had recently married, became pregnant and had a baby. Hebrew grammar is probably the most difficult subject for new immigrant children, and Sarah had shown no particular talent for it, but when she heard that her teacher was home on childbirth leave, she insisted on going to see her. The one thing Sarah knew how to do was to hold infants, and bring them to their mother's breast for nursing. Miri, on the other hand, was completely inexperienced with infants. Sarah showed Miri how to hold her child confidently and naturally, and taught her that her child would not fall apart in her arms. Sarah often visited during her teacher's pregnancy leave, helping her with the initial stages of caring for her baby even as she had helped her own mother.

Then something unexpected happened. When Miri returned to teach, Sarah caught on to Hebrew grammar as if she were a baby learning her mother tongue. Mastering grammar became the key for Sarah to absorbing other subjects as well. Sarah went on to university, where she ended up majoring in linguistics and began a successful career as an academic.

Creating emotional channels through which intellectual content can flow is of utmost importance in teaching. It is as if some aura or whiff of parenthood must accompany successful teaching, and all the more so in situations in which parenthood itself has weakened.

Chapter Nine
The Spiritual Imprint of Parents

Shalom

The guidance of parental figures can continue beyond the journeying and into new stages of the life that are far removed from the original setting. Knowing this can be so is important to all of us, for in our constantly developing and changing society all our children are destined to live in a world substantially different from our own. For years I have pondered the power of parents to continue to inspire their children long after their power and authority – or even their lives – have waned. The story of Shalom, one of the children raised in Yemin Orde, who is now an educator with hundreds of children in his charge, illustrates this.

Shalom was only nine years old when he crossed the deserts and mountains on the way to Sudan. His father, already an older man, was also on this journey, although some of his older siblings had remained behind. His grandmother, whom he remembered as a woman of great piety and virtue, had died shortly before the family left. She had prophesied, correctly, that she would not make it to Israel alive, but that her children and grandchildren would.

Shalom's father struggled to keep the family alive on the journey. In the Sudanese refugee camps, as the Jews awaited the planes that would take them to Israel, many fell victims to diseases that raced through the weakened population. Jewish customs dictate that burial take place on the day of death, but this was perilous because the burials also had to be carried on secretly. If the other refugees knew that there were Jews in their midst, a gravely dangerous situation would have been created. Shalom's father risked his life time and again in order to bring his friends and relatives to burial in a traditional manner. All through this period Shalom saw his father as a hero: strong, courageous and self-sacrificing.

Once in Israel Shalom's father was like a fish out of water. It was difficult for him to adjust to the strange customs of the new land. During the first few months after their arrival, the Ethiopian immigrants were housed in hotels that served as temporary absorption centers.

"They would bring us plates of beef or chicken, but my father and some of the other elders wouldn't eat it," Shalom told me. They felt uncomfortable eating in a massive dining hall, with the food placed on the table for everyone to grab. At home they were the ones to distribute the portions of food in a ritual that reinforced their status. Here, everyone served him or herself, without consideration of hierarchy or custom.

Shalom's father never found work in Israel, and in a somatic expression of his inability to fully adjust to his new life, developed chronic asthma.

"He was an extremely talented man, but here in this new situation, he just sat around and did nothing." But Shalom's admiration for him did not abate. "I used to walk hand in hand with him to synagogue on Saturday morning. I felt that as long as we were together we were surrounded with an aura, a kind of halo of light."

Shalom was attending school some distance away when he felt a compulsion to return home for the weekend. When he arrived, he learned that his father was in the hospital. "I stayed by his bedside the next 24 hours," he explained, "as he fell in and out of consciousness. Early that morning, he passed away."

Shalom, who was entering the 9th grade, was sent to our Village soon after his father's death. It was difficult for him to concentrate. He was obsessed with thoughts of death, and at times, especially when thinking about his father, he would sink into an almost hypnotic trance from which he could be roused only by a loud shout or even a pinch.

One day in late May 1991, Shalom was at home for the weekend when he saw a television broadcast announcing the successful conclusion of Operation Solomon, an airlift in which the 14,500 Jews remaining in Ethiopia – including, presumably, Shalom's older sisters and brothers – had been flown to Israel. The airlift, which had taken only 26 hours, had been kept secret until its completion. Shalom immediately set out to find his long lost family, hitching a ride to the city of Tiberias, where some of the immigrants had been temporarily settled. After a nearly miraculous series of coincidences, Shalom located one of his sisters, whom he had not seen in seven years. Along with her husband and seven children she was housed in a hotel, much as Shalom and his father had been when they had first arrived.

In the excitement of the moment Shalom forgot to inform us at Yemin Orde of his whereabouts. Instead, he offered his services as a translator to the Israeli staff members who were trying best as they could to see to the basic needs of the new immigrants, but felt justifiably overwhelmed in their task. For the first time Shalom felt that he had the opportunity to fill the shoes of his father, who had risked everything to help family and friends during the journey to Sudan and in the refugee camps. There was the feeling of completing a circle; while his father had been made helpless in the new reality of the absorption center-hotels, Shalom was now adept at both the Hebrew language and the strange new customs. Shalom spent the next two weeks helping the immigrants and the staff to understand each other, and when he left, he was awarded a testimonial plaque thanking him for his enormous contribution.

Shalom expected to be disciplined by Yemin Orde for having disappeared for two weeks. Instead, when we learned where he had been, we greeted him as a returning hero and made a point of placing a copy of his testimonial in his personal file.

From that time on Shalom's fear diminished, his concentration improved, and he began to excel at his studies. Life had offered him an opportunity to embody the best qualities of his father in a new situation, in some sense healing the experience of seeing his father's weakness during the period immediately following their arrival in Israel. The ghosts of the past were exorcised, allowing Shalom to draw strength from his father's strength once again. Our Village's contribution was in the dynamic flexibility that is part and parcel of our approach. Our sensitivity to current events, to personal history and to their inter-penetration allowed us to understand Shalom's absence not as an inexcusable breach of trust, but as a potentially unique moment of healing, thus legitimating the spiritual imprint that Shalom's parents left within him.

Restoring the Elixir of Parental Presence

The teenage immigrants from Ethiopia and young refugees from Tibet could not help but make me think about teenagers growing up in the material comfort of much of the Western world. What a contrast the two sets of teenagers presented – the Ethiopians and Tibetans who were eager to overcome all hardship in the pursuit of a new life, and those growing up in middle or upper class families in Europe, America and elsewhere in the developed world. These are teenagers all of us know – the children of relative abundance, seemingly surrounded by everything they might possibly need, from stereos and computers to video cameras and Game Boys. These kids have never had to go to bed hungry or cold, have never felt an immediate threat on their lives.

How many of these teenagers in the midst of this abundance are growing up confused, with no real direction in life? How many parents feel they have lost control over their children's lives and, perhaps even more devastating, have lost the ability to provide their children with guidance and emotional support? How many parents and children, teachers and students are caught in a seemingly unending circle of anger and recriminations, disappointment and crushed expectations? What is blocking and stifling the emotional progress of so many well-to-do children?

The bored and troubled middle-class teenagers many of us know and the Ethiopian children walking through desert and mountains to the Sudanese border are made of the same stuff. For is there really such a thing as a child who has been spoiled, irretrievably gone bad, rotten to the core? Everything I have learned in four decades as an educator tells me that the powers and the zest for life easily identifiable in teenagers caught in extreme crisis are hiding below the surface, even in the most bored and aimless of our young people.

The question, though, is how to activate these powers? How are we to inspire the deep engagement with life that we want for our children? Would the same bored and lethargic teenagers suddenly develop tremendous powers of survival if necessity looked them in the eye? This kind of trans-formation did happen with upper class teenagers from wealthy Jewish families who found themselves in dire situations during the Holocaust. Does it take life-threatening situations to bring out the motivation and resourcefulness in our teenagers?

Middle or upper class teenagers seem to be surrounded by everything they need. But perhaps something is missing from the picture we have drawn.

Something so crucial, so basic, that we take it for granted – although we shouldn't anymore, not in the 21st century. Something that teenagers need like the air they breathe – despite the overt messages to the contrary that they often send us. It is the presence of parents, or parental figures, in their lives. It is that spiritual imprint that Shalom's father left him, those ancestral dreams that powered the Ethiopian teens across the desert and the Tibetan adolescents beyond the Himalayas.

Since Yemin Orde is a children and youth village devoted to residential education, most of the 500 youngsters at our Village have experienced the pain of parental absence or abandonment. We have thus devoted much thought to understanding the nature of the damage to children inflicted by parental absence and what parental presence means. Many books and articles have been written about restoring parental authority over children and adolescents. But our emphasis is not on restoring parental authority, but on restoring parental *presence* – that hard to define elixir that provides teenagers with a sense of guidance as to how to live and be, and the knowledge that the generation that brought them into the world has not abandoned them.

Sammy

The need for parental figures is so indelibly a part of the human psyche that children who have grown up with a sense of being deprived of parental presence often spend a lifetime consumed with anger, as if a great injustice has been inflicted on them. Deep down, children feel they deserve to be raised by human beings for whom being a parent is one of the central tasks of their life. Since one can only come into the world through the actions of others, through their very bodies, shouldn't these others be responsible for showing you what life is about?

I remember realizing the justice of this demand

during one unforgettable incident, as a young man stood outside my home and pummeled my roof with stones. Sammy had grown up without a father, and his mother, too, was more or less dysfunctional. One of his counselors in the Village had apparently suspected him of stealing; Sammy had sought me out throughout that day, in an effort to clear his name. On principle, I try to make myself available to the young people in our Village as much as possible. If I am at a meeting and the secretary is guarding against interruptions, the teenagers know that they have my permission to throw pebbles at the office's back window as a signal that they need to talk to me urgently. But that day I was at meetings away from the Village. Sammy couldn't locate me anywhere. In the evening, at home with my family, I heard tremendous thumping sounds coming from above the ceiling. We both jumped up thinking we were under some kind of attack. Then I heard Sammy's voice. Sammy was throwing, not pebbles, but fist-sized rocks at my roof!

"My father abandoned me," he screamed at the top of his lungs, "my mother abandoned me, and now you are abandoning me," he said.

I wanted to go outside and stop Sammy, but reminded myself of one of the axioms of our educational philosophy: that teenage acting out must be considered a test for us and a cry for help. I realized that this was a moment when I couldn't "do" anything. Sammy's rage was so great that that if I stepped out I might be inviting a rock to my head. I was required to think and to interpret what was happening to me and to Sammy. One part of me wanted to write this young man off as crazy, as pathological, as abnormal. But I pushed aside that impulse. I tried to understand the inner logic of Sammy's deed. The more I thought about it, the more I could see it from his perspective. His anger really was justified. The reality of his life was that he had been virtually abandoned by the generation that brought him into the world. His desire to hold me accountable meant that I had succeeded in becoming a parental figure and thus worthy of punishment. I had become the representative of the older generation, and in that sense, I *was* responsible. I *did* deserve stoning. It was not he who was abnormal and pathological; it was the situation and the world into which he had been born.

Eventually, the boom of the rocks landing on the roof ceased shaking our house. Sammy ran off into the woods. I waited for him to approach me, which he eventually did. He expected me to be enraged with his behavior, and when he saw that I wasn't angry with him, he knew that I had understood something of the nature of his pain. From here on he felt a different kind of trust in me. His extreme action and my response raised our bond to another level, exemplifying the principle that, without exception, even the worst crises are opportunities for new beginnings.

Sammy started to heal, although the process took many years. Memories of his parents could still trigger violence. Several years later, when he was out of our high school and doing the mandatory army service that is required of Israeli youths, he was involved in a fistfight outside a movie theatre, which earned him a police record. The fight was sparked when another young man cursed his mother, thus touching his still open wound.

The story has a happy ending. After the army, Sammy went back to the small town in Israel's north where he had been born. His grandmother, the only member of his family from whom he had experienced love and caring, still lived there. Sammy was determined to make her proud. He decided to become a member of the fire department, with the ambition to become the best firefighter in the town. There was only one problem; his police record made him an undesirable candidate for the fire department. Knowing that our Village remains committed to our young people long after they leave, Sammy asked me for help. I ended up going all the way to the President of Israel, who has the power to grant pardons and amnesties, to get his record erased.

Some months later, Sammy called me. I could hear tremors of exhilaration in his voice. "I just saved my first lives," he said.

There had been a car accident on the highway outside of town, and he had made it to the scene with great speed. He had cut through the door, which had been smashed, and pulled out the two passengers just in time. The car exploded after he had dragged them free.

"I'm dedicating this rescue to you," he told me.

Stories such as Sammy's teach us how deeply parental absence wounds children, and how these wounds can be healed and the feeling of presence restored.

Some of the youth and staff at Yemin Orde Youth Village

Children's and Graduates' Houses are always human scale

The Fred Brenner Arts Pavilion
One of the beautiful buildings at Yemin Orde

Peaceful views are extremely comforting

On the annual cross- country hike – the *Etgar* or "Challenge!"

The synagogue at Yemin Orde

The view towards the Mediterranean Sea from atop
Mt. Carmel at Yemin Orde

A lot of personal time
is spent with the
youngsters.

An Ethiopian teen
enjoys the computer lab.

Youth from
20 countries live
at Yemin Orde.
Here, an
Ethiopian
boy and
a Ukrainian girl.

Adolescents all over the world enjoy soccer.

Young people need an adult presence.

Graduation -A Day of Success!

Chapter Ten
Wholeness That is in Our DNA

Syndrome of the Absent Parent

The Tibetan and Ethiopian adolescents whose lives are so profoundly entwined with those of their ancestors stand in sharp contrast to most children of the 20th and 21st century West. If I had to think of one phrase that could capture the special emotional pain of the past hundred years of Western civilization, I would say that this has been the century of the absent parent.

As far back as 1871, Fyodor Dostoyevsky explored this theme in his novel, *The Devils*, whose anti-heroes are young men and women from affluent families who have grown up with a sense of neglect that ultimately leads them to commit acts of terrible violence. Instead of guiding their children towards wellsprings that can fill the inner emptiness in which their "devils" are incubating, the parents in Dostoyevsky's novel shrink away, fearful of their responsibility, scared, indeed, of the children themselves.

From Dostoyevsky through Kafka and Joyce, some of the greatest modern writers dwell on characters with weak or absent parents – the latest being the American writer, Jonathan Franzen, whose novel *Corrections* depicts grown children of a dysfunctional suburban family abandoning their aging parents as a result of a childhood that left them with no sense of intergenerational connection. I think we can learn as much from these authors' representation of the state of humanity as we can from the testimony of philosophers or psychologists.

Ian McEwan, the brilliant contemporary British novelist, has also portrayed the parental absence in some of his major novels, as the most hauntingly characteristic malaise of the 20th century. In works such as *Atonement* and *A Child in Time* parents are often absent even when they are present, just as in real life. The parents in McEwan's novels lack the moral and psychic presence in their children's consciousness that would enable them to protect their children from the dislocations and corruption that are borne on the winds of 21st century history.

The idea of the parent who is absent even when physically present poses a strikingly symmetrical counterpart to the parental figures just described, who are present in the hearts of their children even when they are physically absent. That is why the syndrome of the absent parent is about much more than physical absence. My own example of an absent parent may be an extreme one. Most parents are not mentally ill, even though our teenage children may sometimes make us feel as if we were. Yet, the central metaphor of absence is a valid description of much of what is wrong with the relationship between parents and teenage children today. Just as my story - and everybody's story – is set, after all, within a historical context, if we are to touch the root problems and challenges of contemporary parenting, we may be helped by becoming aware of the larger story within which our personal stories are taking place.

Search Engine Seeking Parental Wholeness

As a general definition, we might say that an absent parent is one who is unable to bring the fullness of his or her personality into the task of parenting. These parents are incapable of conveying a sense of their world in their relationships with their children, and, therefore, their ability to touch their inner world – the realm bounded by the circle of *Tikkun HaLev* – is limited. This basic deficit is already the starting point for much teenage frustration and provocation. When parents succeed in conveying to their offspring more than one major dimension of their personality, they also are able to transfer the essence of what it means to be a human being. Adolescents have a built in search engine that is constantly seeking parental wholeness, if not signs of expansiveness and greatness, in the human beings who are part of their lives. When the search engine fails to log on to these qualities, frustration and rage begins to brew. And inevitably, the continuous search finds unworthy substitutes.

Many different factors have made the 'absent parent syndrome' endemic in today's world. First, and perhaps foremost, the gradual crumbling of the communal structure in which all human beings once participated has put a tremendous burden on parenthood. At one time nearly everyone lived within the context of a village, close to many members of their extended family. The burden of parenting was not the parents' alone. Grandparents, uncles, aunts and often the entire community were part of the parenting effort.

While in Addis Ababa, Ethiopia in 1990, I remember encountering an Ethiopian Jew who had immigrated to Israel ten years previously. "What are you doing here?" I asked him.

"I came to help my family emigrate to Israel," he told me.

"How many people are in your family?" I asked. I knew that Ethiopians had large families and was well prepared for him to answer "eight" or "ten."

"Eight hundred," was his answer. His concept of family reached back several generations, and, astonishingly, he knew every single member of his clan personally. Raising children within the bosom of such a tribe was a totally different experience than raising them within the constricted, well-defined boundaries of the nuclear family. The circle of the world, a world defined by a vast network of familial connections, affections and obligations, was something that existed naturally.

Can we recreate that circle for our teenagers and illuminate its contours within our shared world? Certainly, many parents, who themselves carry psychological wounds that may be expressed in a feeling of emptiness or alienation, may feel incapable of such a task. Yet, in my experience, the power to parent is something that is almost miraculously self-generating. It is as if this power is called into existence, when an adult takes on the parental mantle and decides to manifest parental presence.

Tulia

Recently, I was reminded once again of the capacity of this mysterious magic called parenthood to appear out of nowhere. Among the latest group of orphans from Eastern European orphanages that Yemin Orde has taken responsibility for raising was an eight year old named Anatoly, or Tulia for short. Tulia's parents died in a car accident in Belarus when he was still an infant. He was placed in a state-run orphan-age. When he arrived in Yemin Orde in 2005, the Russian speaking social worker, who perused the documents he carried with him, recognized his family name, it was a rare one. She had helped take care of an older man and his still more ancient mother, immigrants to Israel from Belarus who shared the same name. Could there be a connection?

When we located the man, in his mid-sixties, and his 87 year old mother, we found that they were, indeed, Tulia's grandfather and great-grandmother. They had come to Israel in order to benefit from the pension and health care services provided by the Israeli government to new immigrants. They had been certain that Tulia was still in a state orphanage in Belarus and had no idea that he had made it to Israel and was living not far from them.

The social worker had remembered them as shut-ins who rarely left the closed circle of mother – who was crippled – and son. They were sad, passive and frightened people. The tiny apartment they inhabited, in a hardscrabble neighborhood in Haifa, was dank and dark. At first they greeted the news that Tulia was in Israel with joy, but quickly, they became frightened that they would be given responsibility for raising him, something they felt financially and emotionally incapable of doing. Instead, we suggested that Tulia would visit them on weekends, but would remain in Yemin Orde during the week.

For Tulia's grandfather and great-grandmother their new role in a child's life sparked a metamorphosis. Painstakingly, they cleaned out a small room for Tulia to sleep in when he came. They bought a lamp and decorated the walls with colored posters, and arranged for a desk and a computer for him. The other rooms of their apartment also began to brighten. So did their faces. Tulia's visits began to be something they looked forward to all week. They even wished that he could spend more and more time with them. Tulia's unexpected reentry into a family circle sped his process of social integration – from the time he began to spend weekends with his family his connection to the Israeli children in our Village improved, as did his language skills and learning.

It was the older generation's transformation, however, that impressed me even more deeply. Before Tulia had come into their lives, they had been feeble and forlorn, despondent, and incapable of running even their own lives. Tulia's presence had brought them to a new plateau of functioning, and bestowed upon them new emotional and spiritual energies. The light of parenthood, I could see once again, is capable of penetrating into very dark places.

The Stream of Life Passes Between Generations

The modern era has created conditions of separation and absence even within the circumscribed contemporary family unit – what we now call the nuclear family. Let us remind ourselves that in the traditional village children could see their parents plowing the fields, tending the livestock or drawing water from the well, and often participated in these activities from an early age. In contrast, the modern work world is a place mostly cordoned off from the presence of children.

At the turn of the 20th century the renowned thinker and educator, John Dewey, warned that the rift that had opened between the world of work and that of family threatened to desiccate the educational endeavor by cutting it off from the natural flow of community and life. This trend has intensified.

During the first two-thirds of the 20th century it was usually only the father who spent long hours at work, and often came home physically exhausted or preoccupied with paperwork and office politics. Now it has become common for both mother and father to work full time soon after a child's birth, and for both to be involved in demanding careers. The specialization that is a feature of modern jobs means that children often don't even fully understand what their parents do in the many hours they spend away from home.

The demands of work and career, and the mental and physical exhaustion that so often accompanies these demands, may cause children to view their parents as one-dimensional, and thus, in a deeper sense, absent. Most of us sacrifice a great deal of our time, our resources and our freedom, in order to raise and support our children. Sometimes this knowledge, along with our inability to imagine an alternative way of raising our children, can cause us to deny the extent to which our involvement in our children's lives is governed by our efforts to be practical and efficient or to find our own forms of fulfillment. We may tell ourselves that our ultimate fulfillment lies in our children's present and future well-being, but too often we do not act accordingly. Much of our psychic energy is wrapped up in organizing ourselves around the need to function in an increasingly complicated world.

Yet, if we are too fully immersed in the demands of an increasingly alienated social and economic world – the world that needs mending – it will rob us of our ability to radiate a fuller presence that can be absorbed into our children's hearts. As parents we can and must develop the ability to separate ourselves, even for a moment at a time, from the stream of life and to relate to ourselves as entities that have that gift of parenthood built into our system. We may indeed feel overwhelmed; we may even experience our own life as shattered. Even so, it is possible, and necessary, to separate my own self-perception, which may be characterized by confusion, despair or incoherence from my sense of myself as a parent. We may think that if we feel a sense of brokenness, this is the only thing we can transmit to our children. That is simply not true. The wholeness of parenthood is in our DNA, connecting us to the stream of life that passes between generations.

Unless we insist on staking out a different kind of territory in our consciousness, by re-adopting a village state of mind as a basic orientation, day-to-day pressures and temptations will tend to triumph over all else in placing their stamp upon our lives, despite our elaborate strategies of denial. Our children intuitively understand when their parents' primary concern is with the ongoing challenges of their work or social life on the one hand, and the technical "management" of their children's lives on the other hand. Such parents are often perceived by their teenage children as external forces intent on imposing their own will and who are always ready to retreat from the distraction children pose to the fulfillment of their adult obligations or desires. In many cases even parents who really do feel that their children are of the utmost importance are forced to surrender to the exigencies of modern life.

Dmitri

The story that follows may seem far-fetched. But it is an example of the way in which good parents can be totally unaware of how what they do for their own survival affects their children. It is intended to be a bold reminder, for those of us who need it, of how necessary it is for a parents to consider the impact of their choices on their children.

One particularly handsome young resident of Yemin Orde was named Dmitri, the only son of a divorced woman who had emigrated with him from the former Soviet Union. Dmitri, however, was reluctant to spend any of his weekends at home with her. After several talks, he finally told me why. Dmitri's mother, an attractive, well-coiffed woman, always had a man in her life, despite her difficulty in forming a long-term relationship. Being with a man, even in a temporary way, gave her a sense of security and well-being. But her son was not part of the exchange – love for security – that she offered her boyfriends.

Dmitri's mother truly loved her son. She wanted to be a good mother, and so she insisted that he periodically visit her on weekends. She cared about his studies, his health and his emotional life. She bought him clothes and cooked his favorite foods. But the walls of her apartment were paper-thin, and she did not clearly think through the consequences of entertaining her boyfriends while Dmitri was at home. The result was that, while he was trying to sleep, he would often hear the moans of his mother and whoever her current lover was; these sounds haunted him. It was as if his mother had two voices that he found difficult to separate, and even more problematic to reconcile: the calm, caring voice of the loving mother and the dark, throaty noises of passionate embrace. The intermingling of these voices confused and disturbed Dmitri. And, in fact, his mother's behavior attested to her unconscious refusal to take full responsibility for her place in Dmitri's life. Her desire to keep a man in her life would intermittently eclipse everything else, making Dmitri and his feelings as invisible as the dark side of the moon.

Could even the greatest dramatist express the inner plight of young Dmitri, whose hormones are swirling and boiling with increasing intensity, as images of sexual passion are superimposed over the likeness of his loving mother? Dmitri's own survival choice was to attempt to separate from his mother completely – thus his refusal to spend weekends at home. Even under conditions of greater stability and privacy than were available to Dmitri and his mother, modern parents are often not fully aware of the way their moods and behavior affect their children.

Have Parents Lost Their Confidence?

We tend to think, or perhaps it is convenient for us to think, that we influence our children only or chiefly through our direct interaction with them. Yet there is a limit to the extent to which we can compartmentalize the lives we share with our teenagers, as the story of Dmitri and his mother show.

The temptation to cordon off our lives into distinct and separate units and functions can prevent real emotional contact from happening even within the family unit. Diversions pull our attention away from each other. We all know that our homes are no longer womb-like sanctuaries, but have been penetrated by electronic connections to the outside world that funnel attention away from children. The time and space in which family members can encounter each other is diminished, replaced by activities like watching television, talking on the telephone or surfing the Internet, in which individuals are transported into realms of virtual experience that are transpiring mostly in their own minds. The American cultural critic Neil Postman, in *The End of Education* and other works, has drawn much public attention through his alarming, even devastating portrayal of the way in which contemporary forms of media have paralyzed and blocked our relationship with our children and our ability to educate.

These characteristic changes in the way people live increase the likelihood that parents will be perceived by their children as absent – as failing to provide the specific quality, the magical elixir of parenthood which teenagers crave. And these quasi-technical explanations dovetail with an even more profound contemporary trend. The syndrome of the parent who is absent even while present can be traced to a widespread loss of confidence on the part of parents in their very ability to be parents. In order to understand this phenomenon at its roots, let us return again to the example of the village – after all, it is in villages or other small communal units that the vast majority of human beings lived for thousands of years.

Within the village the parent's role beyond insuring their progeny's immediate survival was clear: to transmit to the younger generation the wisdom of the past and prepare them to be self-confident members of the community and heads of their own family unit. A significant part of today's parents' helplessness stems from the challenge of fulfilling this task, for which mankind, after countless generations of history, has been innately programmed. Like an incoming tide on a shore full of sandcastles, the modern period, beginning with the industrial and scientific revolutions, has swept away the longstanding attitudes towards past and future that created the context for the relationship between generations. Our lives are, for the most part, not shaped by tradition anymore. The skills we need in order to survive are not, at least superficially, the same skills that our parents and grandparents used. Neither are the accepted values that shape our social lives. As the pace of technological and economic changes accelerates, our view of the past and of the future is blurred like the landscape seen from the window of a high-speed train.

Miriam

The fast moving events that characterize our period can unravel the social fabric from which families draw their strength, thrusting children into paralyzing uncertainty. Take the story of Miriam, a young woman from an illustrious Jewish family that had been living for many generations in Persia, which is now Iran. Miriam's grandfather was a tailor for the Shah of Iran, in charge of a large staff whose mission was to provide the royal court with suitably lavish yet dignified garb. Miriam's grandfather became wealthy enough to invest in real estate, eventually owning seven houses in and around Teheran. Miriam's father was a neurologist with a busy and lucrative practice. Her uncles and aunts on both sides were engineers, merchants and lawyers.

Then two things happened, almost simultaneously. In 1979 the Shah fell, and with him, the family's connections with the top level of the Iranian hierarchy was lost. The position, "Tailor to the Royal Court," and the entire world of pomp and privilege it symbolized, disappeared. Most of Miriam's extended family left Iran for the United States, Italy or Israel.

During this same period Miriam's father was in a car accident, which he was judged by the Iranian courts to have caused. Three women were killed in the accident, and Miriam's father had to pay a huge settlement to their families. All seven houses had to be sold in order to pay for the damage caused by a moment of bad luck.

Miriam's father turned inward, closed his medical offices and agreed to see only a few patients from his home. He grew silent and passive. In the newly tense and mournful household only quarreling interrupted the silence. Miriam's mother and father, who had once lived harmoniously, had begun to fight. All this affected Miriam in an immediate and palpable way. She began to fail at her schoolwork and was unable to make friends in the new school that she began to attend. She felt that her family, which had once seemed open and vibrant, attached to the outside world through a multiplicity of links, had become a sealed room, and that her mouth had been sealed along with it. Since she had been a small child, she had hoped to follow in the footsteps of her uncles and aunts and train as an engineer or medical doctor, but now she began to give up hope in the future. Finally, she decided that her only hope was to leave Iran and her gloomy household, and following an uncle she greatly loved and move to Israel.

Here circles of acquaintance and connection began to turn again in favor of Miriam. A Ministry of Education official who Miriam encountered while in search of a high school to attend was himself from Teheran and knew Miriam's family. Stunned to learn that the family fortune was now depleted, he sent her to Yemin Orde, where I promised her mother, who had accompanied her to Israel, that I would take care of her and give her everything she needed. Slowly she emerged from the shell in which her father's silence had enclosed her. Within the security of our Village she was able to focus her efforts on learning to communicate and create relationships with other young people. Eventually, she regained her lost confidence, and was able to free herself from her father's tragedy and reconnect to earlier, happier familial accomplishments from which she drew hope and ambition.

Center of Gravity within the Global Village

In many ways, the teenage struggle for identity is a struggle to find a past that had become passive and silent like

Miriam's father after the accident. Human beings living in traditional societies often thought of their ancestors as giants. The legendary events of their tribes' collective past resonated with significance and meaning for their own lives. In popular conception today it is the present, with all its attention-grabbing, sense-arousing stimuli and its revolutions in technology and style, that is representative of a fully vibrant life – everything that happened in the past is seen as faded and slightly irrelevant.

The representation of the world as a place whose elements are constantly being improved and made over is at the root of the powerful marriage between technological advance and the consumer society. Western style consumerism, in which products are constantly reinvented and represented as "new and improved," has an effect on parental self-confidence that is potent and widespread. Consumer culture and all that accompanies it has usurped, in important ways, the role that the village and its traditions and elders once filled – the presentation, interpretation and mediation of the world to the younger generation. There is a reason that the spread of Western mass culture to nearly every corner of the world is a phenomenon that is popularly known as the creation of "a global village." Films, television, news shows, magazines, internet, fashion and MTV are part of a single oscillating surface, a colossal distorting mirror, that purports to show young people all over the globe what is important. Mass culture has taken over the function of the traditional village in interpreting and mediating the world and shaping the consciousness of our youngsters.

This might be a good thing, except that the forces that create this mass culture are not guided by the goal of forging and educating human souls. Instead, the form and content of mass culture are tools of the market, a way to sell products through the hypnotic sheen of style and celebrity. The result is that our tools of communication are to a great extent devoted to sending us on a quest for instant gratification. There is little opportunity to escape from the images projected directly into our homes through the television, radio and Internet and into our communities through pervasive advertising. In the face of this tidal wave parents can be forgiven for making the fatal mistake of believing that they have no chance of providing their children with an alternate or complementary structure of meaning.

One of the characteristics of mass media is that it offers itself to us blindly and without discrimination. This makes it nearly impossible for parents to protect children from what is inappropriate for them to see or know at their current stage of development. We can try hard to limit the hours they watch television, or to put filtering programs on our Internet servers, but like the walls in Dmitri's mother's apartment, the protective screens we put up for our children are too thin, and the din of mass culture too shrill. No matter how vigilantly we stand guard, its message will still eventually seep into our children's world.

This is what makes it imperative that we learn to create a space marked by clear contours in which the overwhelming influence of mass culture is neutralized and de-fanged. We do this by drawing within our minds the circle that represents the possibility of changing the world for the better, *Tikkun Olam*, thus reactivating from within the recesses of our memory the world of connectivity and caring which is part of the human legacy. As we become aware of the circle of *Tikkun Olam* we open up the space for a further, deeper, more personal dimension; the circle of *Tikkun HaLev*.

Where am I within these two circles, where is my center of gravity? How can I connect to myself?

The horizontal and vertical lines help me answer these questions. I am a person rooted in my past, moving towards my future; this is the horizontal line. I am a person standing on the solid ground of the present, but my aspirations reach beyond my given reality; the vector of this line is vertical.

The place where these lines meet provides the coordinates of my center of gravity. Using his built-in GPS, which seeks meaning and direction, my adolescent is searching for this center of gravity within me – it is a place he or she can connect to and recharge from, as if from a source of power. The circles and the lines thus position us in a center while marking off an area in which we have regained meaningful influence.

Beyond Authority and Discipline

It is important that we separate within our thinking the concepts of parental presence and influence from the notion of parental authority and discipline. The reassertion of parental influence will not succeed if it takes the shape of mere discipline that is experienced by teenagers as a form of arbitrary authority. Some recent "innovators" suggest a return to the strict hierarchy that once characterized relations between children and their parents and teachers. This kind of thinking should make us uneasy. Is returning to a relationship based on dominance really an option today? Does such a return represent progress, or is it merely a form of retreat and regression? Isn't it possible to take what we have learned about human relationships and our inner worlds and produce something better?

In fact, the depredations of arbitrary authority represent another characteristic sickness of the 20th century. Franz Kafka is, by some accounts, the greatest of modern literary geniuses because of his precise and haunting depiction of modern society. The heroes of his stories inhabit an alienated universe, whose atmosphere is one of vague but ominous threat. Kafka brilliantly depicts the affect on the human soul of a society that has developed a strict bureaucratic structure of control, but has lost its sense of meaning. Joseph K., the central figure of Kafka's master-piece, *The Trial*, is never able to determine the nature of the crime for which he is being judged, and yet is still filled with feelings of guilt and shame up until his very last moment, when he is executed "like a dog."

Kafka's description of the horrific possibilities of modern life was based on his keen intuitions about social and political trends, which seem almost prophetic in light of the universes of totalitarian terror that Hitler and Stalin began to unleash within a decade or so of his death. But there was also a personal and psychological dimension to the desperation of Kafka's characters. The key to this dimension can be found in Kafka's autobiographical *Letter to My Father*, in which a young man tells of his father's tyrannical influence. The father depicted in the book is so obnoxiously domineering that no room remains within the son's psyche in which his own, independent view of reality can develop. Only the humiliating power of the Father's authority holds the world together. In the absence of Father the world would crumble into a million separate pieces.

Chaos is Not Our Destiny

What is the relationship between the alienated world of *The Trial* and the corrosive model of parenting described in *Letter to My Father*? One of the deep truths that emerge from Kafka's work is that the social and psychological worlds – the realms of *Tikkun Olam* and *Tikkun HaLev* – constantly interpenetrate. Parent-child relations based on domination and fear have a toxic affect on a social atmosphere already supercharged with estrangement and threat. But if we succeed in creating a world together with our children where our role as guide or mediator is not arbitrary, but emanates from shared structures of meaning and from a sense of togetherness, we have a chance of rolling back the spread of Kafka's alienated world. Our children will not have the nebulous sense of guilt that makes Joseph K. passive in the face of injustice. They will have an affinity with those aspects of contemporary reality that symbolize the promise of hope.

One thing is sure: our job as parents is made more difficult by the world we are living in today, where all our coordinates, everything that gives us a feeling of stability, are being pulled apart through the force of invisible currents – as if teenagers are the agents or avatars of the chaos that reigns outside the home: through the music they listen to, the clothes they wear, their constantly shifting attention attuned to the latest trends and styles; teenagers often bring the chaotic outside world into the home with a seeming vengeance.

This increases the sense of uncertainty that parents already feel, and creates a chain reaction of anxiety and threat that merges with the fear of potential chaos that is already a constant part of our lives. Especially during these last few decades, when privatizing the economy has become a global catchword, it often seems as if the direction of the world is skewed against community, against sharing. Instead of coming together everything seems to be breaking apart.

Yet the changes in society do not condemn us to recreate impersonality in our own relationships. The world, in all its glittering but alienated forms, does have the power to penetrate inside, into our homes and our inner worlds and even our relationship with our own children. But this is not inevitable. Chaos is not our destiny, even if we have experienced disintegration. *We can come together again.*

Since we can no longer take for granted the support of community, of the clear and precise boundaries that traditional life provided, we have to work from the inside out. We have to recreate the village experience, beginning within our own consciousness. Using the power of our own focused attention and will, we can provide our teenagers with the road map they need and the courage and the wisdom to grow, as they journey into adulthood.

We thus reconceive parenthood or education as an inner task that requires a special kind of consciousness. In order to fully see our children we have to lift ourselves out of the moment's petty but inflammatory conflicts and see how our children's memories of the past and anticipation of the future create their existential present. We have to rise above our own frustrations and re-imagine our children as the center of a unique world in which they are embedded.

The Village State of Mind

In doing this we create a tangible world that we carry within us and which can compensate for the loss of the kind of community that was once the norm for human life. We should take the African proverb, "It takes a village to raise a child," to heart. Yet what a child needs is not the village itself, but the dimensions and values that are embedded in the life of the village – what we call "the village state of mind." The past has a strong presence in the village in the form of the elderly and their life story, in the historical memory carried by the members of the village, in stories about ancestors, and in all the traditional cultural practices. We have to ensure that our child's existential present is anchored in the past just as the village is. The future is present in the village in the sense that the village is a self-perpetuating way of life. Children and adolescents see, in the fabric of daily life, how older children learn skills, are given responsibility and are initiated into the mysteries of adult life, and they know that their turn will come. Our children, too, must feel that they have a stake in the future. Every traditional human culture includes a dimension of "sky," a metaphysical realm of unchanging knowledge and timeless values that bestow meaning and direction to our existence on earth. Our children need a door into that dimension. Earth is the village itself, the place where everything happens. We always have to keep an eye on our children's "earth," the ever-changing conditions of their actual existence.

One way to encapsulate this message is to say that each of us, when raising adolescents, has to recreate the village as an inner state of mind. The global village in which our children are growing up sends messages of fragmentation and threat rather than stability and meaning. Yet, as we begin to understand our children's need for anchors and for direction as they embark on their journey, we can transform the way they see the global village. We can illuminate the environment in which they live, highlighting and accentuating the wholesome elements that parallel those found in a traditional village.

In the face of the tides of the contemporary world, which can sweep from our lives all evidence of the past and annihilate our sense of time as a continuum, we can restore the presence of the past in our children's lives. We can ease the threat our children's experience, because of the uncertain nature of the personal and communal future in our world, by reassuring them that we will be there for them when they need us. We can provide them with a platform that frees them from anxiety and fear and facilitates the dynamic exploration of the world in which they are fated to live.

We create around us an illuminated circle into which our parenting self can grow and expand, thus encircling our children. The story of Enrique illustrates how that circle can be created, if it is absent, or how it can be repaired or expanded, if it is needs mending.

Enrique

Enrique was a teen who came to Yemin Orde Youth Village from destitution in Brazil. His mother, a young woman from an Orthodox Jewish family, had been disowned by her parents after running away with a young mulatto man she had met at "Carnival." When he abandoned her while she was pregnant with Enrique, she was forced to support herself and her infant child by cleaning the offices of a large travel agency in Rio de Janeiro. When Enrique was four years old, his mother placed him in the Lar da Crianca Jewish orphanage. From there he eventually reached our Village in Israel. As part of our efforts to heal and mend Enrique's relationship with his mother, we brought her to Israel for the summer. For the first time since he was an infant, Enrique was able to spend time with his mother in a safe environment. They were able to explore their relationship and iron out the hurt he had felt at her abandonment of him. During her stay, Enrique was able to condense his life and his mother's into one intense summer, as if reliving all that he had missed as a child. It was a summer of turbulent fights and emotional reconciliation. Everyday new wounds opened and old wounds closed. In the Village he had found a place in which his basic needs were taken care of and that implanted in him some sense of security about his future, which enabled him to absorb his mother's narrative with compassion.

When Enrique left Yemin Orde and continued on his life's journey he chose to give me a present: a sculpture in the form of a stone-carved open book, *The Book of My Life*. The letters of most of the first page were black and blurry. Little by little, the letters gained clarity and color, until finally they were bright and multicolored like a rainbow.

"The colored letters represent my life story from the time I came to Yemin Orde," he told me.

Enrique later said, in his usual lyrical way, that for him there are two Yemin Ordes. There is the actual Yemin Orde which, as a graduate he sometimes visits, and there is the ideal Yemin Orde, which he carries around in his heart. He was alluding to a notion he had encountered in a course on Jewish mystical thought.

According to tradition, there are two Jerusalems — one below and one above, the earthly Jerusalem and the heavenly Jerusalem. While the earthly Jerusalem has rocks, roads, buildings and dust, the heavenly one is more of a perfect ideal than an actual place. Still, the two Jerusalems are reflected in each other.

Enrique and many of those lucky enough to have had an adolescence that gave them the opportunity to recover from traumatic childhood experiences carry with them the years of healing and transformation as a representation of a perfect ideal, their heavenly Jerusalem. This new and ancient ideal of the human community as an embracing vortex and crucible is what we have called "the village state of mind."

Finding our parental center of gravity means first regaining confidence in our role as parents. We have to counter the teenager's perception that their parents have lost faith in their own ability to be parents. Once we have overcome the initial shock of parenthood, our small children evoke in most of us an instinctive confidence. We know what to do with them. When they cry, we lift them easily in our arms and hug them until their crying stops. To entertain and teach our little ones we can carry them on our backs to the zoo, watch them as they play on the seesaw, fascinate them with simple fairy tales, sing them lullabies and teach them to read.

With our teenage children we often feel as if we don't know what to do with them anymore. They're too big. They want too many contradictory things. The volume and intensity of their emotions may be frightening. We lose confidence – and they feel it. They lash out against us, testing us, as if thrashing about in quicksand hoping to feel a solid bottom.

Of course even with infants, modern society "succeeded," at least for a time, to weaken our natural parental instincts in a most dramatic way. For several long decades some 20th century "experts" on scientific child rearing convinced millions of mothers that breast-feeding was an archaic practice that was at best primitive and unnecessary and at worst could do permanent psychological harm. Nursing came to be considered, in some circles, something almost obscene, and was banned from the public sphere as if it were a deviant act. Now, of course, we know that mothers pass on to their children much more than just milk when they nurse – both physically, by providing essential components of a healthy immune system, and emotionally. Because we have been convinced of the importance of nursing for a baby's physical and psychological development, parents have insisted on restoring its legitimate place in child rearing.

We need to do the same thing with the parental presence in teenage lives. We need to restore self-confidence in our own instincts, our inner knowledge that our multidimensional presence is of unique importance in our teenage children's development. We need to internalize the knowledge that our job as parents is not finished until our children are functioning adults, and we must renew our belief in our ability to carry the task of parenthood through until its goal has been reached.

Overcoming Separation Anxiety

When our teenagers sense our lack of self-confidence as parents, it heightens their anxiety that we will continue to withdraw emotionally from them. One of the notable insights that the cross-fertilization of psychology and biology has contributed to 20th century thought is the notion of separation anxiety as a guiding emotional principle of the human psyche.

According to John Bowlby, the American psychoanalytic theorist who was influenced by both the disciplines of psychology and animal development, the fear of abandonment is one of the basic components of the psyche of any animal raised by parents. Bowlby's insight was remarkable in its simplicity. Animals desperately need their parents, both for nourishment and protection, and to learn the basics of survival, of how to be the particular kind of animal they are meant to become. Birds, mammals and certainly humans do not learn in a vacuum, but through a close and intensive relationship with a parent. Nearly from the moment of birth, animal and human infants are in a state of distress when separated from their mothers, and they wait anxiously for what Bowlby calls "the safe return of the mother."

This most basic emotion is not something that disappears completely as animals and human beings grow up. The imprint of separation anxiety is so deep that it continues to be a potent force in children, teenagers and even in the adult psyche. Healing separation anxiety is one of the core challenges of *Tikkun HaLev*, or fixing the inner circle of the heart. Separation anxiety morphs into many forms and appears as a factor in nearly every kind of relationship. In the relationship between parent and teenager the separation anxiety of each side feeds on that of the other side. Teenagers fear parental abandonment. At least part of the meaning of provocative teenage behavior is that the teenager is testing the parent in order to affirm or negate their worst fears; namely, that their parent will reject and abandon them.

Parents, for their part, also often fear abandonment.

They fear that their children will reject them, or are already in the process of rejecting them. This fear connects with the fear of abandonment they carry with them from infancy, a fear that is a ubiquitous part of human development, but which has been complicated by the myriad of negative experiences most people endure as they grow up. Part of becoming the kind of parental presence our children need in their lives means overcoming our fear of rejection and separation. The fear of rejection and separation is part of what keeps us emotionally withdrawn from our teenager, just as it keeps them provoking and testing our commitment to them.

Acting In Versus Acting Out

To a great extent, then, adolescent "acting out" is a response to the lopsided equation between abandonment and maternal return in the world they are growing into. There is far too much abandonment – divorce, anomie, unpredictable change, parental absence, breakdown of community – and far too little embrace and reassurance, which are the elements of reality that could represent for the teenagers the safe return of the mother. The sense of a reality flooded by abandonment maddens teenagers, makes them strike out blindly at the generation that brought them into the world, but has retreated from their responsibility of providing guidance in how to live.

In the face of teenage acting out parents have to learn to "act in." Expanding our presence in our teenagers' lives does not mean reacting to provocation with threats and punishments. Instead, we have to turn inward, at least initially, becoming aware of our own power, and the possibility we have to counter absence with meaningful presence, emptiness with content, and abandonment with embrace. In order for any of this to happen we have to allow ourselves to be touched inside by the challenge of parenthood. We have to understand that the parent-child relationship is not a one-way street. On a deep level our teenagers offer us a chance to mine our own souls, our own history and our own convictions in order to bring ourselves fully into the parent-child relationship.

Not least, through our teenagers we receive the opportunity to reach back into our own teenage years. Learning to become aware of the circle of *Tikkun HaLev* in the context of parenting, we attend to our own shattered hearts. If our teenage years were troubled, we have the chance to heal ourselves. We can do this by focusing our inner awareness and achieving enough understanding so that we do not reproduce our own negative experiences, passing them on to our children. If our teenage years were good ones, we cannot simply take it for granted that our children will have the same experience. We have to tap into that goodness, and transmit it to our children.

Chapter Eleven
Garden of the Late Bloomers

Children Never Give Up on their Parents

The inward journey we need to take as parents is not psychological but relational. It will not focus on the isolated individual psyche, but on how our inner experiences and emotional depths touch those of our children, and vice versa. That is why I believe it is important to share what I have learned about the significance of parents in the eyes of their children from years of experience directing a Youth Village for children from disadvantaged or immigrant populations. Many of the teenagers in our Village come from families plagued by divorce, abandonment or violence. Quite a few are children from the former Soviet Union who, because of their circumstances, have chosen to come to live in Israel without their parents. Others are the children of Ethiopian immigrants whose parents never fully adjusted to life in Israel, are chronically unemployed, illiterate and speak only a broken Hebrew.

One might think that as Director of the Yemin Orde Youth Village where, I am often forced to take on a quasi-parental role, I would have developed a perspective in which the importance of biological parenthood is diminished. Some educators, including some I admire, have adopted such a view. A.S. Neill expresses disdain for parents in his classic book, *Summerhill.* Neill's ambition at the Summerhill School was to create a school community where children could be safely detoxified from what he considered the often poisonous influence of their parents. I think that Neill was right about some important things, for example, his belief in the primacy of children's emotional life over intellectual achievement as a goal of education and his emphasis on liberating children from fear. But on the issue of parents he was dead wrong. We are used to talking about paternal and maternal instincts, but there is at least as deeply rooted an instinct within children's hearts that keeps their relationship to their parents important, almost regardless who the parents are. As an educator in a Youth Village, my position has given me a unique vantage point from which to perceive the hunger of children for their parents. If there is one thing I have learned during my years as an educator, it is how profoundly parents figure in their children's mind and hearts.

It is important for parents and teachers to realize that children never really give up on parental figures. This may come as big news to some of us, because teenagers are notoriously hard on their parents. During the years of adolescence, rebellion and independence are part of the teenager's basic developmental agenda. It is commonly known that teenagers test themselves and their newfound power against their parents and often challenge their parent's authority and beliefs. What is less well known is that while all this is going on, somewhere in the depth of the child's psyche, the connection to parents, the purity of children's love and admiration for their parents and the deep desire to make parents proud never fades. This insight must be carved into the hearts of everyone involved in raising or educating teenagers.

We can illustrate this through the story of three roommates, two Eastern European immigrants and one native Israeli whose parents represented the most severe kinds of absence and dysfunction, and yet who refused to write them off.

Ivan

First, there was Ivan. His father, married to another woman, had impregnated his mother in Russia, and had moved to Israel shortly afterwards. Fifteen years later Ivan came to Israel and enrolled in Yemin Orde, never having met or heard from his father. Over the next year Ivan searched for his father, only to be told by the Ministry of the Interior that his father was dead and buried in a cemetery in central Israel. Ivan went to the cemetery, and after searching for hours, found his father's grave. On the grave he placed a note inside a clear plastic cover to protect it from rain, saying that he was this man's son and that he would welcome contact with anyone who knew him.

Six months later, he received a phone call from his half-sister, already married and with children of her own. Neither Ivan nor his sister had known about each other's existence until she had found the note on their father's grave. Ivan and his sister became very close friends, and spent hours talking about the father they shared, whom the sister had known well. Together, they "reconstructed" the father, giving him new life through their discussions. Ivan's search for his father, and the portrait of his father that he was eventually able to piece together, were important steps to solidify his own sense of identity.

Yaakov

Ivan had a roommate, Yaakov, a strikingly beautiful young man, who had also spent his childhood in Russia. Yaakov's father and mother had divorced when Yaakov was eight. His father, on the verge of immigrating, offered to take Yaakov to Israel with him. Like many eight-year olds, Yaakov was attached to his mother and decided to stay with her. His father treated this as a grievous insult. Yaakov's mother eventually died, and Yaakov moved to Israel and Yemin Orde. But his father refused to see him. Yaakov would travel to the town where his father lived – a two-hour journey – and knock on the door. His father would open the door, see his handsome son and then slam the door on him. Remarkably, Yaakov refused to say a bad word about his father during all our discussions with him. As much as I found his father's behavior abhorrent, I was amazed by Yaakov's loyalty. Not even total rejection could extinguish the flame of love he held for his father.

Eli

Ivan's other roommate was an Israeli named Eli, whose mother had been committed to a mental hospital after numerous psychotic episodes. Eli's story is the most complicated, both because he was the most troubled of the three roommates and because his love for his mother was submerged below the surface of his personality for a number of years. As a child, Eli had been passed around from the home of one relative to another, until finally he landed in our Village. Periodically, Eli's mother would escape the hospital wards and arrive unannounced on the grounds of Yemin Orde in search of her son, eager to make sure that he was doing all right, and wanting to talk to me and to his teachers to ensure that he was progressing in his studies. Her clothes were disheveled and saliva often dribbled down from the side of her mouth onto her chin. Eli would run away every time his mother arrived. After she left, he would almost invariably engage in some kind of destructive misbehavior. He liked to set fires, to steal and to talk back to teachers.

Soon after Eli came to our Village, I told him my "secret" in a conscious effort to form a bond between the two of us. My mother, too, had been insane. This knowledge formed the basis of a covenant of trust between us. Subtly, through the tone of voice with which I spoke about my mother, I tried to convey to him that loving an insane mother was a legitimate, even a healthy, choice.

Eli could always get to me when he needed to talk, and even though his behavior often bordered on madness, I saw that there was a basic element of goodness and normalcy in his personality. His friends trusted him – and in some strange way, I trusted him as well. Sometimes, when he seemed to be particularly agitated, his counselors feared that he might do himself or others harm. He seemed to sense their worry and he would seek me out.

"You don't have to lose any sleep tonight over me," he would say. And I would believe him.

In Yemin Orde, the twenty residential houses where the children sleep and live are each named after a great figure from Jewish or general history. Eli lived in the Abraham Lincoln house. One day his counselor called me and told me to quickly come to the house. When I got there, I saw what Eli had done. In huge letters he had painted alongside the name Abraham Lincoln House so that now the sign read Eli Mousayef House.

I was secretly pleased. To me Eli's massive graffiti meant that he really did feel at home in the Village, and also that he had dreams of greatness. Along with discussions of the seriousness involved in damaging communal property, and our insistence on Eli repairing the damage he had done himself, I managed to slip in a line that showed him that I recognized and affirmed his dreams. "Someday there *will* be a Eli Mousayef house," I joked with him.

A year or so later came another incident that further tested our relationship. Eli was in the habit of attending school and synagogue services intermittently – only when he felt like it. I had given his counselors and teachers instructions to let him sleep in when he felt like it. One Saturday morning, our Sabbath, while nearly the entire population of the Village was in synagogue for Sabbath prayers, someone had tortured and beheaded a cat. Its burnt and headless carcass was found as we walked back from synagogue. All signs pointed to Eli as the perpetrator. His mother had made one of her dramatic appearances in the Village just the day before, and aside from her disturbing demeanor, the counselors knew that Eli came undone after nearly every one of his mother's visits. As soon as Eli understood what had happened, and that he was the prime suspect, he ran off into the woods surrounding our village and disappeared.

The staff believed that Eli's flight was another indication that it was he who had slain the cat, but something about the whole story didn't make sense to me. I had never seen that kind of cruelty in him and I didn't believe it existed. After the staff had searched for him for a whole day in the forest, I went out carrying a bullhorn.

"I know you didn't do it," I announced. "I know you didn't do it."

Almost immediately, I found him. He had camouflaged himself in a pile of leaves, but had responded right away to my faith in him by emerging from his hiding place. As it turned out, Eli had not tortured and killed the cat. This terrible act had been carried out by a visitor, the brother of one of our resident youths, who had run away from a drug rehabilitation program and come to Yemin Orde for refuge.

The next year, his senior year, Eli began to emerge from his cocoon. Like someone waking up to bright sunlight and realizing that he had missed the early train to work, Eli saw his friends taking the matriculation exams that would qualify them for college or university, and realized, as if for the first time, that actions carry with them long term consequences.

He came to me in a state of despair. "I've missed my chance," he said, "It's too late."

What would have happened to him if I had

conveyed to him that he had, indeed, already missed the train? That his life could no longer be a success story? I sometimes refer to our Village as a garden of the late bloomers because so many of our teenagers – like so many teenagers – are wrapped in cocoons, dealing with traumatic childhood experiences and healing from them during the early years of adolescence. Only later are they capable of devoting themselves to building their future. The trick is to be there for these teenagers when they are ready to bloom.

"This year is an important year," I told Eli. "If you work hard this year, we'll help you catch up."

Eli did work hard, and became a member of our first class at the *Mechina,* a gap-year program that was designed just for our late bloomers, enabling them to make up study materials they had missed and prepare for the mandatory three years in the Israeli army. It was as if all the energies that seemed to have been wasted during Eli's teenage years had actually been stored up inside and burst outwards now in great abundance. Eli succeeded in his studies, and at the same time took on enormous responsibility – organizing the buying and cooking of food for the entire 45-person program.

At the end of the year the *Mechina* youth take a long and arduous hike, concluding with their arrival at their graduation ceremony. Eli's mother was there to greet him as he finished the hike, carrying the giant flag, exhausted but exhilarated from the effort of the walk, and from the effort he had made to transform his life. This time he did not turn away from his mother, though her appearance was as jarring as ever. I was near enough to hear their conversation, which was touching and heartbreaking at the same time.

"Here's 50 shekels ," his mother said, shoving the money, the equivalent of about $10, into Eli's hand. "Remember, you owe me 50 shekels." And then she added something else, as if from a different layer of her persona. "You're the most precious thing in my life," she said softly.

He took the money. "Mom," he said. "I owe you a lot more than 50 shekels."

His voice and eyes gave clear evidence of the love for his mother that he had hidden all these years, hidden until he was strong enough to face her. For me Eli's words and expression were evidence of the powerful, perhaps genetic instinct that draws children to their parents and keeps them from rejecting them despite almost any circumstance.

Guardians of Shattered Dreams

Rural Ethiopia is a society in which parental authority over their children is nearly absolute. Here in Israel Ethiopian parents are disempowered. The skills they bring with them from Ethiopia are little appreciated here in Israel; they often survive by receiving government aid. Children thus see parents who were once respected for their resourcefulness, wisdom and mastery of their environment drift into passivity, collecting welfare checks and developing psychosomatic diseases, like Shalom's father did. Yet, it is rare to find an Ethiopian youngster who does not retain a deep and basic respect for his parents and elders. Many times I have seen Ethiopians who are already members of street gangs with police records enter their parent's home and be transformed. Dreadlocks, earrings and all, they will hold their right forearm with their left hand and bow slightly, while extending their right hand to their parents in the Ethiopian gesture of respect.

For example, I will never forget the sight of Naftali Fantahon bending his head to kiss his father's knees during his graduation ceremony from the Technion. Naftali is one of the first Ethiopians ever to graduate as an engineer from Israel's highly prestigious college of science and technology.

Naftali's father came to the graduation dressed in his traditional white clothes, an elderly man who never learned to read or to write even in his own language. Kissing his father's knees was, for Naftali, a gesture that honored his father as his source of life and origin.

I remember another youngster who never knew his father. His mother was so retarded that she didn't have full control over her swallow function, saliva dribbled down her chin. He was a beautiful and talented young man, who bloomed into promising young adulthood here at Yemin Orde. And yet his mother was always a central part of his dreams.

"Some day I am going to get an academic prize, in university," he would often tell me, "and my mother is going to see what sprang from her."

Where do children get this intense desire to share their triumphs with their parents, no matter who their parents are? To me it seems that children are the silent guardians of their parents' shattered dreams. They carry, as if in their genetic code, their parents' unfulfilled potential.

Flies on the Wall

Raising teenagers can indeed be exhausting and frustrating, and can often leave us feeling like a failure. We naturally tend to think that the arguments, insolence, rebelliousness and day-to-day manipulations of our teenagers tell the whole story of what they think of us. In actuality all of these conflicts, though important, are secondary phenomenon compared to the place that teenagers reserve in the depths of their heart for their parents. If we could be like flies on the wall and hear our teenagers talking about us to their friends, often times we would be in for a pleasant surprise, because it is so different from the insolent assessments of us which they sometimes throw in our face. It is as if children instinctively know what our religious traditions teach: that parents are partners with God in the creation of the world – the unique world of each child.

The hidden reverence of children for their parents is almost a religious feeling. Jewish commentators have long noted that the first part of the Ten Commandments deals with religious devotion – the belief in one God, the prohibitions against idolatry and blasphemy, and the commandment to keep the Sabbath day holy. Perhaps for this reason "Honor thy father and mother" is part of the first half of the Ten Commandments, which focus on the human being's relationship to God, rather than the second half, which is about man's relationship to his fellow man. This built-in place in their children's hearts puts parents in a position of tremendous responsibility and provides an amazing opportunity. Parents who do not truly wish the best for their children do exist, and they have the power to draw their children towards destruction with an almost black magic force, as I have witnessed more than once during the course of my career.

As the stories we've recounted show, parents are virtually never failures in their children's eyes, and parents who recover their good will towards their children will always get a second chance. Children, except in extreme cases, are always waiting for their parents to come through, are always willing to give them a chance to rehabilitate themselves as parents, because their unconscious need for parental figures is so profound. Children are willing to pay a high price, risking deep disappointment, if there is chance to renew contact or trust with a parental figure.

Salmon Swimming Upstream

The instinct drawing adolescents towards parents is so strong that when it is frustrated, children look for substitutes. My own healing in adolescence involved such a search. First, expressing a desire to draw closer to the

Jewish religious tradition, I asked my grandparents who had always been an island of sanity in my world if I could live with them so as to attend school in the heavily religious area in which they lived. Some of the children in the new school I had chosen sensed the weakness of my family background and began to scapegoat me. But a child named Simcha Fenster befriended and protected me, and brought me home to his parents.

Whereas the Nazi persecution had indirectly caused my mother's mental breakdown, the Fenster family's experience during the holocaust was, remarkably, a source of strength for them. The Fenster's had escaped ahead of the Nazi occupation of their hometown of Bratislava into the wilderness. They had carried their young children on their backs as they moved from hiding place to hiding place. Because they felt a sense of gratitude and triumph at having been able to stay together as a family, they miraculously emerged from the Holocaust as whole people. I could feel this in their household, which was homey but also aesthetic, orderly and sweet smelling, suffused with values, but also with pride in the family and what it represented. Mrs. Fenster was noble, delicate and very natural in her appearance and her manner. She and Mr. Fenster took a special interest in me.

Simcha had decided to attend high school in Kfar Haroeh, a religious boarding school headed by a charismatic rabbi, Moshe Zvi Neriah. When I decided to attend as well, Mr. Fenster went with me, acting as a surrogate parent. I remember clearly, as if engraved on my heart, the sight of Mr. Fenster carrying my battered suitcase for me towards the boarding school. The suitcase, upholstered, with stripes, represented for me my wanderings in search of a home. It was as if, in Mr. Fenster's small gesture of carrying my suitcase, he had lifted up my past – all the painful memories I carried with me – and transformed them by sharing their weight, thus breaking the taut cords of my loneliness.

In Kfar Haroaeh I met other surrogate parents. One was Rabbi Menachem Ofen, who had organized religious services right in the midst of a Nazi death camp, fasting on the Day of Atonement even though he was nearly starving. He, too, carried my suitcase – this time, when frustrated and angry with the school and with myself, I had walked to the main road dragging my belongings with me, intending to leave Kfar Haroeh forever. Rabbi Ofen ran after me and with sweetness and determination attempted to convince me not to leave. Finally, as I stood not knowing what to do, he picked up my eternal suitcase and carried it carefully back to my room.

Another influential surrogate family during my high school years at Kfar Haroeh was that of Zvi Weinberg, a history teacher with a passion for his subject, exacting and yet full of sharp humor. Together with his wife, Sitta, he was raising nine children. Mr. Weinberg had the mentality of a mentor, of someone for whom every encounter in the classroom was an occasion for transmitting not just knowledge, but a way of thinking. The emotional boundaries between the classroom and his home were porous. I knew very early in my experience in Kfar Haroaeh that what I was really looking for was family, not institutional life. The Weinberg home was a living connection for me, between the life of the classroom and that of the family, open and stimulating enough to make me feel like I had indeed found a home. In fact, seven years later I married their youngest daughter, Shuli, and we eventually had five children of our own!

It is rare, though, for teachers to replace parents in children's hearts. I recall my own search for parental figures as something with the strength of an instinctual drive, like that of salmon swimming upstream to the place they were born, or birds migrating to safe shores for the winter. The force of this drive is something that all parents would do well to remember.

The teenage struggle against parents is often so fierce that the parents might come to believe that the teenagers actually want to see their parents defeated, humiliated or dislodged from their place in their children's lives. But, deep down, teenagers want their parents to survive their onslaught. The defeat of a parent is a Pyrrhic victory for a teenager. Teenagers want their parents to be strong, even as they demand the right to reveal their own strength by testing it against that of their parents. Shifting the way parents and educators see their teenagers will empower them enormously, and allow them to survive the teenage onslaught. This shift of vision involves seeing the total context of teenagers' lives, and developing a new perspective of their role as guide and touchstone for their children.

Small Umbrella, Big Umbrella

Returning to the comparison with raising small children, it seems that most adults are able to channel the best part of themselves into that effort. They feel a natural flow of love emanating from their hearts towards their small child, expressing it externally with embraces and kisses. They often scrape the rust from their creative tools and energies in the service of creating a happy childhood for their young ones. Single mothers, for example, who do fine in raising small children because they trust their parental instincts, may begin to falter when their children transform into teens whose consciousness of the world widens.

With small children we need a small umbrella in order to provide them with the feeling of safety they need to develop. With older children – teenagers – we need a larger umbrella, a context of interrelationship that has been consciously broadened. The parent needs to radiate self-confidence as the mediator of the big things: the past, the future, the certainty that life has meaning and is proceeding, ultimately, in a good direction. The function of the parent is not to be an expert in all kind of theories, but to allow the adolescent to feel that he is walking purposefully on solid ground.

No Vacation From Parenthood

Too many of us take a kind of vacation from parenthood when it comes to our adolescent offspring. We suffer the illusion that adolescence is a finish line marking the end of our concentrated parental efforts, or that we no longer need to supervise our children's every move; they now have the capability of seeing to many of their daily needs by themselves. For our part the effort of raising small children has left us fatigued, without even being conscious of it. Our lack of confidence in our ability to effectively guide our teenagers to adulthood amidst the chaos of the outside world combines with our teenagers' own often misinterpreted demand for independence. We decide to let them be, and convince ourselves that we are doing the right thing. After all, we tell ourselves, isn't independence what teenagers need? Don't major elements of our culture extol teenage freedom?

Even if we don't take a leave of absence from our duties as parents, we often put our worst foot forward. If parenting small children brings out some of our best qualities – patience, love, compassion, tenderness – it sometimes seems as if the opposite is true when it comes to our teenagers. Our worst attributes are activated. We lose patience and blow up in anger. We are easily offended, and take things personally. We don't know how or what we have to give.

We need to internalize our awareness of our task, which is to offer our adolescent children a vision of wholeness and possibility – in short, to show them what it means to be a human being. Regaining faith in the centrality of our role as parents, we will find it simpler to return to our natural parental instincts. Instinct usually implies something done almost automatically, like breathing. In this case, however, we are talking about returning to an instinct that has been largely lost. Awareness and intention are thus the key. The kind of awareness we need to cultivate has two aspects to it. One aspect is awareness of our teenager and the journey from childhood to adulthood that he or she is on. Without understanding adolescence and its developmental path, we risk wandering in the dark as parents.

The other is awareness of ourselves in relation to our children. Since what we are teaching our children is how to live, we can transmit nothing that is not already alive in us as parents. All of us, to a greater or lesser extent, suffer from psychological wounds, from feelings of brokenness or despair. But we can choose, utilizing the power of our inner awareness, to relate to our teenage children from the healthiest and most wholesome part of our being, just as we usually do when we are with small children.

We have to employ both these modes of awareness simultaneously if we are to transform awareness into intention, making parenting a conscious activity in which we understand what we are doing, and really mean it. To act effectively and meaningfully as a parent or an educator means learning how to collect and focus the disparate parts of our personality.

Chapter Twelve
Embracing a Second Birth

The Changed Meaning of Adolescence

The life of a young Ethiopian boy living far from the city in a traditional society was quite different from the regimented and protected life of most teenagers in the West. From the age of 12 a boy like Tedesse, our young math student, might be given responsibility for a flock of sheep. For several weeks, he would wander with the sheep in a circular route through meadows and over hills, seeking fresh pasture and sources of pure water, exploring the countryside, experiencing his independence, and testing his own physical skills and powers of judgment against the elements.

Yet at all times Tedesse would be connected to the traditions and expectations of his culture. His adventure would take place within the context of service to his family and his village. The wool, milk and meat that the sheep he kept alive were essential for the survival and well-being of his people, and as such, also would provide a place for him in life. Often, in village society, young men and women were married off to each other between the ages of 12 and 16. But rather than start a fully independent household, they would move in with either the bride or groom's family, beginning their life as fledgling adults within the protected circle formed by their elders.

Our understanding of teenagers today will be enriched if we compare the context in which we now live to the traditional world that preceded it. The structure of our psyche has not radically changed. The emotional needs and expectations that have developed over thousands of years of human civilization were not suddenly erased by the abrupt and rapid spread of urban, industrial society. Emotionally, we still live in expectation of the structures of meaning and community that have accompanied the development of human life from time immemorial.

To a great extent, adolescence, as we know it now, is a phenomenon of the modern world. Whereas in traditional society sexual maturity, marked by various kinds of rites of passage, began an entirely new period in a person's life, the industrial revolution caused an extension of childhood for an additional period of 5 to 8 years, beyond the onset of sexual maturity. At first, this lengthening of some aspects of childhood was confined to the upper classes. These classes understood that if their children were to retain their privileged place within the emerging social structure of the modern world, they would have to undergo a longer period of learning and honing of skills.

For a long time adolescence and the concept of secondary school education that accompanied it were solely upper class phenomenon. Teenagers from the lower classes worked from an early age – in factories, farms or as apprentices to craftsmen of various kinds. Eventually, at least in the West, as democracy and the demand for equal opportunity spread, child labor was outlawed and secondary education began to be accepted as a norm in all sectors of society. To this day in developing countries child labor is common, and often, in lower class families in Western society, adolescents – especially young women – bear a greater share of responsibility for the welfare of the household then do teenagers from more privileged homes.

Adolescence, then, has drastically changed in meaning over the last few centuries. It has come to designate a period when physical and mental powers are highly developed, but familial and economic responsibilities remain, basically, that of a child's. This state of conflicting status – again, mainly for Western teenagers – is another major source of the obsessive search for identity that has come to characterize the teenage years in Western society.

Societal changes have in many ways created adolescence as we know it. Still, the period that followed the physical and sexual maturing of a child has always had a special status. In the Talmud, a compendium of law and ethical and spiritual teachings that was recorded by Jewish sages some 1500 years ago, children are considered adults when they reach sexual maturity; for boys, on the average, at the age of 13 and for girls at the age of 12. According to Jewish law, a 13 year old who damages property, murders or commits some other offense can be held fully accountable in the courtroom. But, the Talmud adds, this is not the case under divine law. Human courts must prosecute teenage offenders, in order to maintain the social order. But God recognizes the moratorium of adolescence. Only from the age of 20 is a person liable for punishment from heaven for his misdeeds.

In ancient society teenagers married, worked and took on responsibility, and thus had to be held liable for their actions. But from the perspective of heaven, teenagers are still children in the process of forging their soul.

In the Kabbalistic corpus of the 16th century Safed School of Jewish mysticism the beginning of the teenage years are likened to the embryonic period before birth – they are literally termed "a second period of pregnancy." Adult consciousness is present in the early teenage years as a kind of seed that must be nurtured and developed. Only when parents feel confident enough in their offspring's grasp of reality to allow them to serve as agents in managing the family's financial resources (usually around the age of 20) is full adult consciousness considered to have been reached. As we shall see, this Kabbalistic idea is strikingly similar to the thinking of some modern psychological and educational thinkers.

Teenagers are Outcasts

Before the invention of modern adolescence, the early teenage years were a time for self-discovery. This is still the case in the rural areas of non-Western societies today. In contrast, the teenager growing up in a contemporary urban family will very likely miss out on the formative encounters such as Tedesse, our Ethiopian shepherd boy, experienced. They will have little opportunity to feel the thrill of exploration or the emotional solace of connection to tradition. For the Ethiopian boy living in a pastoral society such as Tedesse's, the knowledge that he is contributing to his family's well-being is an important factor in his developing self-confidence. He is earning the trust of his elders and is succeeding at a task that is important to his entire tribe; he thus has the feeling that he is carving a place out for himself within society.

Our own teenagers, for the most part, are not partners in the struggle for economic survival or success in which middle or upper class families are engaged. If anything, with their constant demands and desires, teenagers have become to their parents a disturbance or distraction and source of almost constant tension. More than once children have been placed in my care by their parents who, to my absolute amazement, told me that they simply don't want them around. In Yemin Orde, these children were from second or third generation immigrant families who had sunk into impoverishment.

I can still see in my mind's eye the horrifying image of an invalid parent waving his cane at his frightened child as he drove him into my office, yelling after him, "If you ever come back to our home, I'll throw you into the neighborhood garbage bin."

We know quite well that rejection in various forms – not always so direct or brutal – is not confined to families in circumstances marked by misery. The longstanding upper class tradition of sending even small children away to boarding schools, if the purpose was to give them a better education, evidences subterranean currents which have little in common with those stated aims.

With the trend of sending children away so embedded in Western culture, have we really yet learned to make a home together with our teens? Teenagers can feel deep inside that they are outcasts even when remaining at home, and thus behave accordingly. Whether the current challenge for a modern couple is succeeding in their careers or keeping their marriage alive, having a teenager underfoot is something that can often feel like an extra, unwanted load. And teenagers, with their super sensitive emotional antennae, can feel the tension in the air. They feel the disruption that they cause within the adult world, actually experiencing it magnified as in a distorting mirror.

In contrast to Tedesse modern teenagers do not have the freedom and the independence to explore their surroundings, to wander unimpeded through new territory. The modern urban world is too populated, too rough and dangerous, too circumscribed by private property and public laws, to allow a teenager to disappear on his own for a few weeks. Often, what is left for the child is to sink into a kind of intoxication with "things," objects which attempt to create an aura of adventure or which provide the teenager with a sense of identity and connection. These items may be clothes, movies, music or computer games. All are ready-made for consumption and do not, in any real way, advance the teenage search for self-discovery.

Holistic Parenthood

Can things be otherwise? Can modern families and teenagers experience a "return to nature," in which adolescence once again becomes a true coming of age, in which young persons can discover themselves while discovering the world and can find themselves by learning to track their own progress on the journey of life?

This can happen only if, as parents and educators, we learn to look at our adolescents in a holistic way. In the field of health and medicine there has been a huge movement towards healing methods that rely on the natural healing powers inherent in each person. In contrast to modern medicine, which has come to rely on more and more highly advanced technologies such as microsurgery and magnetic resonance imaging, natural healing methods are usually low tech and rely on processes and formulas which the patient himself can participate in executing.

One of the fascinating aspects of the Ethiopian presence in Israel is that many Ethiopians eventually make trips back to Ethiopia in order to receive health care from healers using traditional methods. This is despite the fact that in terms of modern medical science, Israel is one of the most advanced countries in the world and Ethiopia is one of the least advanced. There are just some diseases, especially chronic illnesses, such as asthma, arthritis, and mental illness, which seem to respond better to traditional healing methods more than to the most advanced scientific techniques. This may especially be true when, as often is the case, there is a psychosomatic element to the illness.

The most common critique that practitioners of holistic health techniques make of scientific methodologies is that they tend to focus on a particular part of the body while putting less emphasis on the way all the different parts of the body interact with each other. Often, the emotional and spiritual aspects of illness, which are often keys to the process of healing and recovery, are ignored. The strength of holistic health care lies in its emphasis on the total person, and on the way the body, mind and spirit all affect a person's physical health. If twenty-five years ago the medical establishment mostly looked at holistic healing as a form of fraud, today more and more hospitals and health insurance plans recognize its efficacy and offer alternative treatments alongside mainstream therapies.

Can we transplant some of this same spirit of holism to the field of education? Educators today are armed with an array of methods and techniques that deal with learning skills and learning blocks, with fine motor ability and attention deficit, with emotional disorders, abnormal behavior patterns and a host of other specifics. There are times when these techniques are imperative and can make a great deal of difference in a teenager's life. But these techniques are mostly based on a fractional perspective. They focus on isolated components of a child's life. What about the child's totality? What is the total context of the child's life?

Holistic parenting and educating means returning to the most basic components of the human experience. It means understanding that the modern, urban, industrial world, rife with alienation and often bereft of community, should not be our automatic point of reference in dealing with children and adolescents. It means that as parents and educators, we have to attempt to reconstruct, in our children's lives, some of the structures of meaning, support and direction which existed for so long in human history.

Gabriel

Gabriel was an Ethiopian immigrant with a problem shared by many teenagers, although rarely with such a degree of severity. Gabriel had acne. Not just a few pimples, but an outbreak that made his whole face look like an area of volcanic activity, with mounds of angry red blemishes topped with tiny eruptions of white pus.

Compounding Gabriel's sensitivity about his appearances was the fact that during this particular time in Israel there was a great deal of media attention devoted to the possibility that some of the new Ethiopian immigrant population had come to Israel bearing AIDS. AIDS was known to be epidemic in some of the impoverished urban centers of East Africa. The Ethiopians, in the months preceding the Operation Solomon airlift, had spent up to a year living in conditions of squalor in Addis Ababa, where the percentage of the population carrying the AIDS virus is high.

Some of the men undoubtedly had engaged in sexual relations with women from the local population. Other members of the Beta Yisrael community were infected when they used the services of "shot doctors," traditional healers who added the hypodermic needle to their array of treatments. Many Africans have an almost supernatural belief in the power of shots because of their collective memory of their first, miraculous introduction to antibiotics. Unscrupulous and unsanitary healers take advantage of this reverence. Somehow, Gabriel connected his severe acne with AIDS. This might have had its source in the feelings of repulsion that both AIDS and his acne evoked. Or perhaps Gabriel had made some kind of subconscious association that made his acne seem leprous, like the impurity invoked by AIDS. Maybe the knowledge that AIDS can be transmitted through blood, and that his blood seemed to be 'boiling' to the surface of his face contributed to his fixation.

One fine morning, I was urgently called to the area of the water tower, where Gabriel had been caught attempting to commit suicide by leaping from the top. I brought Gabriel into my office, and learned for the first time that he was obsessed with the idea that he had been infected with AIDS. To my own astonishment I did something that I might not have done if I had stopped to think about it with a team of psychological experts. I grabbed Gabriel's face, and began to lick his boils with my tongue, I looked him in the eyes, and said: "Would I have done that if I thought you had AIDS?" My unspoken message was more important than my verbal reassurance: If you have AIDS, my actions said, then I am willing to risk getting AIDS too. You are not alone in the world, whatever your problems are. I am willing to share your very blood.

The story of Gabriel is an example of our holistic approach. Instead of answering Gabriel's concerns about his acne with an informative lecture about how AIDS is contracted or manifested, I plunged in symbolically, demonstrating to him with my whole being that he did not have to be afraid. Once I allayed his fears we could deal with the treatment of his acne problem. If I had just sent him to the school nurse, his secret fears about his safety, security, place in life, etc. would not have been addressed. Gabriel as the whole person needed my help; not just his acne.

From the moment of that encounter Gabriel's psychological status improved. His acne eventually healed and he went on to graduate successfully from high school, to serve in the army, and to start a career in public relations and media. My response – to plunge into a quite repulsive act in order to demonstrate how linked I was to his agony and fear – gave Gabriel a feeling of connection that he needed with the adult world. This enabled him to continue his path towards independence. Today, he is outstanding in his capability of giving to others.

More than an Extension of our Ego

Participating in the raising of the next generation, either as a parent or an educator, is one of the most momentous and meaningful activities possible in a human life. Because parenting is so common an experience, so much part of the fabric of everyday life, we often tend to depreciate its significance. Yet is there any other endeavor in which we have to give of our self in such a profound way, not intermittently, but on a day to day basis over the course of many years? If we are to sustain the psychic energy that will allow us to do this, we need to nourish ourselves with ideas as well as techniques. That is why, before entering into a more practical discussion of adolescents and the challenges their upbringing raises, let us take a moment to reflect again on the root nature of our task.

In spite of all we have read and have absorbed about raising teenagers, it is never superfluous to remind ourselves that teenagers are people, and our relationship with them deserves to be founded on principles equal to those we have adapted as mature people towards humanity as a whole. Whatever we understand as decent and selfless in our relationship with others applies with teenagers too.

The Talmud tells us that every person is a world onto himself. Thus, "He who saves a single life, it is as if he had saved the entire world." As in Gabriel's story, there are many ways in which to save a human life. Each human being is unique and each life is of infinite value. This insight is something that we often forget in our dealings with teenagers, especially if they are our own. For the corollary of the power we have with our children by virtue of our being their genetic fore-bearers is the responsibility we have to see them as more, much more, than an extension of our own ego. This is one of the most crucial and most difficult aspects of parenthood: to develop the ability to see our children, even while realizing their dependence on us, as the center of a world of their own.

Encircling is Embracing

It was Martin Buber, one of the most acclaimed Jewish thinkers of the last century, who articulated a different way to relate to other human beings. Buber taught that our primary way of encountering the divine was through our relationship with other people. He said that human beings had two basic modes when relating to others: I-It and I-You. In the I-it mode, I relate to others as if they were objects. I can analyze them. I can manipulate them. I can catalogue their strengths and weaknesses, their limitations. I see them as separate from myself.

In the I-You mode I encounter the totality of the other person with my whole being. Deactivating the force field that we often use to strengthen and delineate our sense of separateness, I realize that together, through our encounter, we are both part of something new. Our meeting, if it is real, creates something that is more than the sum of each of our individual consciousnesses. In a true meeting between two individuals, the relationship is not *within* each person, but *between* them.

What is most real for Buber is the trans-individual – the spiritual world we call into being when we really face each other's uniqueness and infiniteness. We need to intend this meeting with the full power of our will, with our own inner identity. Once we do, we are changed. During those moments of true meeting, we are part of something larger. In encountering another person we create, through our embrace, a living world of which we are both part. Buber calls this kind of meeting "encircling."

Perhaps the best way to make this idea concrete is to use an example we are all familiar with: romantic love. Lovers create their own unique world that they share together, a world with its own language, geography and history. Buber's great insight is that every authentic encounter between human beings shares some of this same quality. One could say that the intentions of the people within an encounter create the laws of nature that govern the world that they together create.

When two people speak truthfully together, they

create a shared world whose quality is honesty and truthfulness. When people refuse to categorize or manipulate each other in their encounters, they create a world that is not fragmented by objectifying definitions or defined by the quest for power. When people remember that the other person is unique and infinite, a world onto themselves, the "laws of nature" that is created are such that the totality of the other person, beyond what can be seen with the naked eye or expressed in one discrete moment, can unfold.

Our Teenager's Future Mode of Being

From the time I began to think of myself as an educator, these teachings became my main source of inner guidance. Since then, I have been consumed with the question of how to apply Buber's teachings in a practical and transmissible way to real interactions between people, especially during the formative age of adolescence. As parents and educators we are entrusted with teaching our children what life is. Beyond the specific skills, concepts or languages we want our children to learn, we have to teach them something much more basic: how to be in the world, both in relation to themselves and in relation to others.

Our primary method of teaching our children how to be is through our relationship with them. This is their lifeline, their oxygen. Essentially, what they experience coming from us is what they will be able to inhabit as a mode of being in the future. If our teenagers feel compassion and patience emanating from us as we face them and their dilemmas, they will become familiar with the world as a compassionate place and will learn to be patient and compassionate themselves. What we give to them at one stage, they will internalize and embody at the next stage. The quality of our relationship with our adolescents shapes and forms the inner structure of their world.

The Adolescent as Embryo

Let us now take a more focused look at that special stage in life called adolescence. Like the *Kabbalah*, the renowned psychologist Margaret Mahler, in her extensive writing on teenagers, has compared adolescence not to childhood but to a much earlier stage of development. Adolescence, she says, is like a "second birth." In biological birth, an infant is born into the circle of the immediate family. In adolescence, with biological growth moving towards completion with the onset of sexual maturity, the child is reborn into the social world as an infant, or even embryonic, adult.

One corollary of Mahler's idea of a "second birth" is that adolescence is a new start, during which traumas and wounds from childhood have a chance to be healed. Another, even more basic insight we can glean from Mahler's concept is that adolescents, no matter how independent they seem or say they want to be, are like infants who have to learn how to sit up, crawl, and stand before they can walk. If healthy adulthood is characterized by independence and individuation, Mahler's idea of a second, psychological birth in adolescence means that we have to be aware of the enormous level of support that teens need to achieve such adulthood.

Following the lead of educational philosopher Samuel Hugo Bergman, a contemporary of Buber, we can compare the fledgling adolescent to an embryo who survives and grows because it is hooked-up to its mother's blood system. During pregnancy blood flows through the mother into the embryo and then back again to the mother. Even after the child is born, he or she has a great need to be held by their mother, to sleep near her, to gain nourishment and even antibodies from her milk.

A Tumultuous and Dynamic Process of Unfolding

By imagining the teenager as an infant, we don't mean to deny the obvious teenage need for independence. The teenage demand for independence should be respected, but should not influence us into relinquishing the same profound sense of responsibility for a child's welfare that we have when raising an infant. We must recognize the years of adolescence as a formative period with its own developmental stages. Theoreticians have mapped the developmental stages of infancy with great precision during the last 100 years. No one expects an infant to walk before it can stand, or to speak before it can walk. And although the crying of a six-month old can be annoying, to say the least, the vast majority of us are wise enough not to yell at or strike an infant as punishment for crying.

As parents and educators, we must internalize the fact that the adolescent journey to adulthood works itself out through a developmental path, and that the different forms of acting out and rebelliousness which our teens display are in no way representative of the final configuration their personality and behavior will form. Our teenagers are works in progress, living through a tumultuous and dynamic process of unfolding. We must preserve our awareness of this constantly within our hearts and minds.

Metaphorical Continuum

Earlier we noted the widespread return of mothers to nursing as an example of the resurgence of a virtually instinctual practice that "scientific experts" on child rearing attempted to uproot earlier in the 20th century. An even more radical example of a return to holistic child-raising methods is presented in the book, *The Continuum Concept*, by Jean Leidloff. Based on observations of the child rearing practices of South American tribes living in inaccessible jungle areas, particularly the Yaquna, *The Continuum Concept* offers a practical response to John Bowlby's theories about the ubiquitous presence of separation anxiety in the human psyche that we cited earlier. Liedloff made several interesting observations. She noted that in the tribal villages she visited infants are carried around almost constantly by their mothers or another adult. The infants nurse when they want to, and spend much of their time slowly assimilating all the components of daily life – the smells of cooking, the sounds of the jungle, the wetness and current of the river – all the while feeling totally safe against their mothers' familiar skin.

In contrast to modern infants, Liedloff observed, Yaquna infants rarely cry. The central, repeating dynamic in a modern infant's life – the disappearance of the mother and her reappearance triggered by crying – is foreign to the lives of the Yaquna infants. According to Liedloff, Yaquna toddlers, rather than developing a higher level of dependency on their mothers, are far more independent than their modern counterparts and learn earlier to play alone for longer stretches of time. Liedloff's assumption is that all human beings used to raise their infants in the way that the Yaquna do, and that infants emerge from their mothers' womb expecting to spend the next year and a half or so in almost constant physical contact with their mothers. Infants don't need to be the center of attention sometimes and ignored at other times; they need to be quietly present at the periphery of their parents' attention all the time. By the time they are toddlers, Yaquna infants have grown accustomed to the world as a place in which they feel at home. According to Liedloff, they grow up to be calmer, happier human beings, whose personalities do not bear the scars of separation anxiety and the apprehensive wait for "the safe return of the mother."

The continuum concept applies, at least

metaphorically, to teenagers as well. We need to carry them around with us to a far greater extent than we may think. Just as the Yaquna strap their infants to their body in order to carry them around comfortably, we need to augment our teenagers' constant, unconscious sense of security with our physical presence. In the case of teens, what they need is not the constant physical touch of our bodies, but a form of easy, unconditional emotional availability. They need to know that they can get a quick hug whenever they need it. They need to be reassured that we will not abandon them, and that we are with them for the duration.

Whether every detail of the observations and theory propounded in *The Continuum Concept* should be considered literally true is beyond our ability to judge. But we do know that for a good part of human history people lived in small hunter-gatherer tribes, sharing almost everything and passing down the wisdom needed for survival from generation to generation. Later, for the thousands of years since society began to organize around agriculture, most humans have lived in villages united by common goals and traditions. Geographically, the area in which people lived had boundaries and characteristics with which everybody was familiar. Information from other parts of the world traveled slowly, and often never penetrated one society from another. There was a high level of contact and commitment between the generations.

The Aura of Togetherness

It was in this context that human emotions and our inner sense of security developed. Yet while the world has changed, the need for a structured world with defined contours has not. Can teenagers, our "infant adults," learn to gain the confidence to independently explore their surroundings and the possibilities that life offers? They certainly cannot do it without a sense of support and community. We need to offer them an aura of togetherness, a sense of inner coherence and emotional solidarity that defies the swirling chaos that surrounds us. We must recreate, intentionally, through the messages that we constantly broadcast to our children, the sense of belonging and togetherness that once defined human existence.

If we put together the Buberian idea that two people create a world together with Mahler and Bergman's image of the fledgling adolescent as an embryo and infant, we begin to arrive at a picture of the intense level of involvement our teenagers need from us. This involvement, as we shall see, is not necessarily one that will take up huge blocks of our time. Adolescents need to feel their freedom, and need to spend much time with their peers. But we do need to create a bond with our teenager that is like a shared blood system, a shared world that involves our very essence. The I-thou relationship means that the parent or educator we must face the adolescent with the willingness to carry him or her psychologically at the moment when he or she needs, like an infant, to be lifted up.

In order to create a working tool for our educators, who are constantly dealing with children from broken homes and broken worlds, we have created within Yemin Orde Youth Village our own catalogue of images. These images represent the ideas that form the core of our educational philosophy, and include the two circles introduced earlier called the circle of *Tikkun Olam* (mending the world) and the circle of *Tikkun HaLev* (mending the heart). Buber's idea of "encirclement" and Bergman's notion of creating a shared bloodstream with our child add an additional dimension to our image of the circle. We had previously described the two circles as tools for broadening the conceptual horizon of our parenting to include an awareness of human history and contemporary society, for focusing us on the deep and often unconscious emotional struggles of adolescence, and for better understanding the interrelationship between these two realms. Now we see that the image of the circle is not only an image of awareness, but of connection. A la Buber and Bergman, the circle symbolizes the shared world we create in our relationship to our teenagers, and the existential bond that links us together in our role as parents and mentors.

The circle linking parents and teenagers is a circle of love, commitment and community, a circle that teaches that the world is not a place of isolation but of profound connectedness. Can we defy the conventional wisdom of our era, in regards to raising children and adolescents, in order to create the aura of togetherness they need? Starting as far back as Dr. Spock's famous *Baby and Child Care*, first published in the early 1960s, we have been told that if we are too supportive of our children we will create dependency in them. Especially in the United States and other places influenced by this ethos of self-reliance, the message we have been conditioned to send to our teenagers is "We may be taking care of your needs right now. But soon enough, you'll be out there on your own. And then? You had better be strong, because it's sink or swim."

The Paradox of Independence

Isn't this the wrong message to give? We have to help our children grow wings that will allow them to fly. However, the way to accomplish this is not through messages that magnify the sense of fractured-ness and shattering already so characteristic of our modern society.

One prevailing response to disciplinary problems, used almost instinctually by both schools and parents, is to invoke the threat of abandonment and separation. If a teenager is acting out – which most healthy teens will to some extent or another – many parents will threaten him or her with some form of "shape up or ship out." This might mean telling the adolescent that he or she will be sent to boarding school or some kind of quasi-military summer camp if he or she cannot abide by the rules of the home. In educational settings, the threat might be expulsion, a tactic developed in order to foster excellence and create elite groups by 'weeding out' disrupters. In both cases, disapproval is conveyed through a withholding or severing of emotional connections.

Yet what these tactics do is to merge, within the teenager's mind and experience, rebellion and the threat of abandonment. Since rebellion is one of the teenagers' main tools for testing their strength and independence, this strategy actually serves to hurt a teen's development towards healthy independence. One possible outcome is that the teenager will curtail their rebellious instincts because of an anxiety over separation, thus leaving the feelings originally expressed by acting out smoldering and unresolved. Another possibility is that a teenager's rebellion will be fueled by the perceived cruelty of a world whose code of justice is based on the threat of abandonment.

In general, the cult of independence is closely connected to the modern capitalist ethic that mythologizes the idea of "the self made man" who has "pulled himself up by his own bootstraps" (try it – it happens to be impossible) and made it without help from others. With all due respect to the amazing accomplishments of capitalism, no human being ever makes it in the world without help. I have sometimes had occasion to see what I consider to be the psychological results of the current orthodoxy of the American myth of self-reliance. Typically, successful, workaholic fathers will attempt to foster independence in their children when they are in their late teens or twenties. "Now you're going to have to make it on your own," they tell their sons or daughters. Sometimes they will give them some money and send them away to another city, state or country. They believe that by having their children make their own way in the world they will increase their self-confidence and strength.

Hard work is very important. But in these cases, parents' unstated but clearly heard message to their children is not about the value of hard work. It is that we are living in a dog-eat-dog, every man for himself world; a world in which children cannot rely on parents. One can often read the psychological results of this message on the faces of the children. They may be proud of their parents and of the efforts they have made to make it on their own. But beneath the surface, their voice, and the expressions on their faces tell another story. Children of successful parents who have demanded that they "make it on their own" often betray wounded-ness and a lack of true inner confidence. Even if they have become successful, these children are often far from emotionally secure and happy.

The irony, of course, is that the first generation of successful businessmen have often hailed from a more traditional home, where immigrant parents had provided a potent model of emotional commitment to children. Their nearly penniless fathers would never have given them a few dollars and told them to scram, as they did to their own son. And so they took the strength of their father's love and unconditional commitment with them into the business world or professional world, and were enormously successful. But their own children, the third generation, became victims of the gospel of self-reliance applied in a misguided way, and never really achieved the kind of emotional self-confidence that would allow them to radiate the power and independence that their parents did.

But aren't we responsible for teaching our children how to survive? Of course we are. However, the sink or swim school of building confidence in life is founded on a basic misconception. Human beings by nature are not parasites that must be forcibly weaned from a natural preference towards dependency. Teenagers want to become independent. They want a place in the world, an identity they can call their own. They want to become active, honored contributors to society. They want to arrive at the stage when they can make their own decisions, trust their own judgment, and have the power to navigate in directions they choose. Like plants, which grow in the direction of sunlight, the natural tendency of teenagers is to be attracted to independence.

But plants, in order to grow towards the sunlight, need soil and water as well as sun. And among the nutrients that children need in order to develop towards independence is confidence in the future. They need exactly the kind of confidence that is undermined by questions such as "What will you do when I am no longer here?" or statements like "When you are 18, you're out of the house and on your own." This kind of message amplifies the threat of an already threatening world. Instead of encouraging our teens to make for the open seas, the threat of loneliness, separation, and failure will send them scurrying for safe shores. Our anxiety over the possibility of future dependency will inevitably be interpreted by our teens as fear of the world, fear of the future, or lack of confidence in their abilities.

It may sound paradoxical, but the real message teens need in order to move towards independence is not "It's a rough world out there and in just a little while, you're going to have to sink or swim." Instead, they need to hear "I'm with you now and I will be with you in the future. I will do everything in my power to make sure that your life is successful." This is the embrace, the interconnected bloodstream, the shared circle of fates that our infant, embryonic adults – that is to say our teens – need from us. Just as infants raised by parents who carry them around constantly learn more quickly to play and explore the world by themselves, teens surrounded by reassurances of togetherness will reach a fuller, more solid independence. If they feel our embrace, they will be able to internalize us, to carry us around with them into the future, as a source of confidence and strength. And, through the world we create together, they can learn that the larger world "out there" is not composed of just separation and loneliness, but also of warmth, togetherness and commitment to each other. This can only happen if we keep intact our capacity to connect with this simple truth, which challenges much of what passes for wisdom in today's world.

Assuming Normalcy

Every September, for the past 30 years, hundreds of teenagers begin another year of their lives on our mountain at Yemin Orde. Every day, 365 days a year, 24 hours a day, the stream of life continues here. Still, the start of the new school year, along with the Jewish High Holy Days, marks the lives of the teenagers; a new year is a new start. Every school year we are confronted with the need to integrate new educators, in particular counselors, into our staff. Counselors are usually young men and women in their early twenties – often just out of the army and some of them Yemin Orde graduates themselves – who are on the front lines of our Village's educational endeavor. The counselors are each charged with supervising the daily life of a specific group of youngsters who live together in one of our many houses. They are often the ones who have to deal in real time with the nearly constant flood of tiny crises, blow-ups, and emotional oscillations that characterize adolescent life. Because of the pressure and intensity of their task, combined with their relative youth, counselors often experience emotional "burn out" – thus the relatively high turnover rate that translates into a continuous need for training seminars.

Every new school year thus confronts us with a crucial and perplexing question. Is it possible to almost instantly transform these young educators for the work they will be doing with teenagers? How can one distill experience into a language that is not just theoretical, but practical, flexible and effective enough for the shifting circumstances of day-to-day life?

Don't parents, to a great extent, participate in this same dilemma? Although they may not think about it in this fashion, aren't parents constantly in need of finding new energies — a way to renew themselves in relation to their awesome and frustrating role? Once we have learned to internalize the need to prepare ourselves intellectually, emotionally, and spiritually for the task of parenting, the next step is to ask: What kind of conceptual tools should we employ in this attempt at self-transformation?

This question has been asked ad-infinitum over the past 100 years. An explosion of guidebooks for parents written by "experts" of various kinds has attempted to answer it. At least once every decade, trends and ideas have changed and a new generation of child-rearing books has gained favor. Sometimes it seems as if the plethora of guidebooks is actually a direct indication of the diminution of parental confidence, a retreat from the natural relationship between parent and child to be found in more traditional societies.

One sign of this retreat is the prevalence of psychological language and concepts in the modern discourse on child-rearing. Is our goal to supply parents with this specialized knowledge so that, in some cases, they can replace psychologists in the therapeutic role? The answer is obviously no. A person who has not trained as a psychologist, under expert supervision over a relatively long period of internship, should not assume he has become one by reading a book. Psychology should be left to psychologists, who should be utilized only in cases that suggest pathology. Psychological therapy takes place in a special environment, one step removed from everyday life. But parents and educators need a way to navigate the natural flow of life they share with their children. This may, in the end, diminish the number of times that intervention from a psychologist is needed, but it is something very different from urging parents to become para-analysts by practicing models and theories used by professional therapists.

The psychotherapeutic terminology that has become part of common parlance can also help us clarify the difference between the kind of help therapy offers and the kind of involvement in children's lives we are advocating for parents and educators. In the world and the language of psychotherapy, "containment" is a central motif. In recent decades, psychotherapeutic language has penetrated into daily life through 'psychological' call-in radio and television shows and popular paperback 'how-to' books. Nowadays, people speak about "containing" each other as if it were a natural mode of relating, not part of a professional terminology. It is as if we have all become para-psychotherapists, especially where children and adolescents are concerned.

Ideally, in the process of containment the therapist empties himself of his own concerns, and turns himself totally to the task of listening, leading the client towards new insights about himself. The notion of containment may have its place within the specialized context of therapy, with its intensely focused fifty-minute slots of time. Yet, in everyday life is 'containment' a realistic option?

Rather than containing our teenagers we should strive to encircle them, which as Buber and Bergman's thinking suggests, is something that comes as naturally to us as an embrace. Our goal should be to produce a shared circle that marks the boundaries of our shared fate, rather than a containment that may reek of a built-in hierarchical relationship in which one side has all the enlightenment and the other side all the pain and confusion.

Containment is also something that is nearly impossible to do during the course of everyday life, at those odd and often stressful moments when parents and teachers encounter children. One of my close friends is a child psychologist. It always fascinates and amuses me to see how he is with his own children – no different from the rest of us, sometimes losing patience, and certainly never engaging in the kind of thinking and behavior he does when doing therapy.

What we are interested in is bringing ourselves to our children "as is," in the midst of life. Our emphasis is not in seeing the pathological, abnormal side of adolescence. It is normality we want to focus on. Hasn't the time arrived for us to reassess and broaden our notion of what is normal? If we assume that our teenagers are normal, and that their behavior, though challenging, makes sense within the context of their journey to adulthood, doesn't that stand a good chance of becoming a self-fulfilling prophesy?

Chapter Thirteen
Feeling Earth

Intoxication and Punishment

Village traditions are of major importance in molding group coherence and building up individual character and identity. Our annual program includes several long treks through nature, the climax of which is our 106 kilometer long walk from sea to sea – from the Sea of Galilee to the shores of the Mediterranean – which graduating seniors undertake.

This year, after the steep and rough climb from the Valley of Jezreel to Mt. Carmel, three of the youngsters sneaked away from where the others rested, made their way to the nearby town of Daliat al Carmel, and returned with several bottles of vodka. During the last part of the hike, which culminates with a ceremony and celebration, including fireworks and fire-writing in which the whole Village participates, the three arrived completely intoxicated. They pushed their way to the stage, and in front of the stunned audience one of them grabbed the microphone from the MC and began to drunkenly address the crowd. Before the whole Village, he lamented that he had no father to appreciate his achievement in finishing the hike. Still reeling in his drunkenness, he also began to expound on the values he had learned in the Village – values which he was now, in his view, trampling.

The other youngsters, who had worked equally hard to complete the hike and to produce the festivities, rushed the stage in fury.

"What are we, a village of drunkards?" they said. It took a while until things calmed down, but when they did, the Village youngsters demanded justice, feeling that their much anticipated special occasion had been ruined.

After a sleepless night, the natural leaders of the seniors decided to take responsibility. "It is not only them, it is us all who should be punished," they said, "We should not have allowed this to happen."

They concluded that the most appropriate punishment would be to repeat the cross-country hike, and do it this time with dignity until the very end. When offered alternatives to this punishment – we wanted them back in school – they responded with sharp objections. "This is not just. You are lousy educators!" they exclaimed.

The following weekend, to our profound anxiety, the two seniors, who had protested most vigorously that the punishment of repeating the hike was the most appropriate one, disappeared. They arrived at our gates on Sunday, worn out and covered with dust. They announced that they had backed up their declarations with action, and had just returned from completing again the 106 kilometer hike, thus rescuing their own dignity and that of the entire senior class.

Although this story could be interpreted in a number of ways, the youngsters referred to their repetition of the arduous hike as a self-inflicted punishment. Their concept of punishment reflected what they had imbibed during their years in the Village. Punishment emerges from insight and self-choice, is connected to the recovery of integrity and dignity, and includes suffering. Yet it also includes, when you get to the bottom of it, achievement, if not satisfaction.

Nothing That Sounds Like Rebellion Really Is

It is virtually impossible to raise or work with adolescents without at some point dealing with the issues of discipline and punishment. Adolescence is a time of rebellion, although the extent of that rebellion – how long it lasts, how extreme and unyielding it is – will be influenced by the kind of parental presence a teenager feels in his or her life. Rebel-lion is natural, but it becomes pathological when it is so powerful that it overwhelms every other aspect of development. Teenagers whose consciousness is colored by the multidimensional presence of a parent will not need to test reality as intensely and radically as other teens. If parents and educators have managed to open their children to the flow of time and to some form of transcendence, their feeling of being trapped within a narrow consciousness whose constricting shells they must violently crack through will be far less pronounced. When parents and educators provide an emotional bridge to the world of adults, teenage rebellion loses its pathological edge.

Part of the adolescent search for identity involves testing the limits and rules that they see as imposed from without; rules that do not have to do with them and their inner feelings and impulses. In fact, children and adolescents do not fully grasp the most basic rule of life, that of causality. They do not yet fully understand the fact that actions have consequences. Rebellion is a way of experi-menting with the laws of causality while testing their own strength, and testing the strength of the significant adults in their lives from whom they receive guidance.

Adolescents have a sharply developed intuition that allows them to hone in on the weaknesses of both the systems of rules in the home, school, or society they are living in, and the specific weaknesses of their parents, educators, and other adults. That is why teenagers succeed so often in enraging us. But although it often seems as though our teenagers want to destroy our authority, this is not their intention. They want to give us their best blow, and yet see us standing strong. Our ability to respond wisely to their provocative behavior restores their self-confidence in us as models and guides.

We don't usually understand this, at least not during

those moments when we are being tested. We tend to see our teenager's acting out, extreme language and defiant behavior as a personal insult and as an expression of his or her deepest feelings about us. We feel teenage rebellion as a rejection of the wisdom and values that we are attempting to transmit to the next generation – and thus as a mark of personal failure. Experienced in this way, teenage insolence and defiance becomes a painful and almost intolerable blow to our own self-conception and self-esteem.

It is a mistake to think that the dialogue ignited by the tensions between us is the real dialogue that is going on. This is where the framework of the two lines and two circles can help us. *(Diagram on Page 65.)* The horizontal line running between past and future helps us remember that the interaction that is taking place right now is part of a far more extended story that began in infancy and will end in adulthood. The vertical line points to the fact that every interaction, especially those that have the potential to explode into verbal or even physical hostility, will be seen by teenagers as a test of our ethics and ideals. Are our ideals strong enough to keep us calm and give us presence of mind even when we are provoked? The circles, perhaps most importantly, call our attention to the depth dimension of our child's psyche, reminding us that what is happening on the surface is only the tip of the iceberg. The two lines and two circles can help us organize our mindset around the insight that nothing that sounds like rebellion really is rebellion.

Although our children have a rich inner life, their emotional vocabulary is limited, their ability to express feelings in words not yet fully developed. Teenagers are generally dualistic in their perceptions; they often see things, including relationships, in black and white. They are manipulative, without necessarily being conscious of their manipulations. However, we should not allow our adolescents to set the psychological and moral tone of our encounters. We cannot afford to regress to the manner or lingo in which a teenager might speak to us. We have to lead them forward. We have to understand that the voice of rebellion is the voice of testing, of trial and error. It is not the adolescent's inner voice. We must never allow ourselves to attribute evil to them. Everything they do, unless they damage or endanger others, should be interpreted as an expression of their feelings, within a vacuum of unconditional acceptance.

The teenager's message will be one of separation, "I don't want to see you, I don't want to listen to you, I reject your values and your rules."

Our response should be to perceive him or her as part of a circle that includes our own self. Their message of separation should be met by a message of inclusion. When it is time for me to respond to rules that have been broken, or lines that have been crossed, my commitment should be to the child in question, not to the rules.

On Punishing as an Insider

Even when we have to punish, the message we should give to our teenagers is that their efforts to break away, to test us and their independence, will not cause us to abandon them. Yes, we do have to set limits for our teenagers. They need and want limits. And yes, we do have to correct behavior that harms them or others. At the same time, we have to take care not to use punishment as an opportunity to clip our adolescents' wings. We need to avoid sending the covert message that their efforts to separate and become independent will cause us to cut them off from us. Often, when we are challenged, we are quick to subliminally flash the threat of abandonment. We do this because our teenagers evoke within us the feeling that their behavior is a threat to the system we live by. We then punish out of fear. In reality, the only fear we should have is of responding from our own panic and wounds. Fear and hurt can cause us to take our eyes off the ball, distract us from our goal, which must always remain the good of the adolescent. We do, however, need to punish sometimes.

Matti, an immigrant child, steals from his roommates, from the Village offices, even from the museum gift shop on class trips. Obviously, this kind of behavior cannot be tolerated, because it is anti-social at its roots. We need to use punishment as a tool to weaken Matti's desire to steal, otherwise his behavior will continue and will likely escalate, ultimately bringing disaster down upon him. Attending to the problems that Matti expresses through stealing will take much more than punishment. But punishment is necessary also for its public dimension; in order to affirm and underline acceptable and unacceptable norms of behavior.

How should we punish? One of the main lessons our work in the Village has taught us is that one must not punish in an emotional vacuum. Punishment must be in the context of a relationship. There are many reasons that teenagers misbehave. We've talked about their desire to test their strength, independence and the significant adults in their life. But there is always an element of pain in negative behavior. This pain stems from hurt and anger over the unresolved wounds of childhood and the confusion and threat emanating from an uncertain future. In order to punish you first must have a connection to the adolescent's pain – to be his or her partner in dealing with pain.

The way to do this is by connecting to an adolescent's inner feelings, their intimacy. What is it that he or she is ashamed of? What is he or she proud of? What are they hiding? What are they afraid to speak about? He or she may be missing a pet cat that died or that their parents gave away. Or ashamed that they have not yet begun to develop physically the way classmates have. He or she may be proud of their musical ability, or the way they do their hair. The place where an adolescent is wounded, the source of their anger and frustration, and thus misbehavior, is on the inside. Therefore, you must punish him or her as an insider, from a place of *Tikkun*, of insight. It is forbidden to punish someone for whom you are not an insider, part of their "intimacy." You don't necessarily have to verbalize the knowledge that makes you an insider. But you do need to connect, in your own consciousness, to your adolescent's inner feelings and struggles.

Punishment should not be perceived as coming from a stranger, nor from someone who is making his or herself into a stranger by hardening his or her heart in order to punish. A teenager should see punishment as coming from someone who cares.

Meaningful Punishment

Another rule of thumb at Yemin Orde is that there should never be a punishment which does not have an element of choice in it. This means that punishment must always be preceded by dialogue and negotiation. From the adult perspective dialogue is an opportunity to turn misbehavior and punishment into a trigger for insight. Presenting some kind of choice in punishment allows a teenager to maintain his or her dignity, and to feel that he or she is not simply being bullied by a dictator or victimized by an arbitrary system. Dialogue, negotiation and choice nourish the part of the teenager that is expressing the inner drive towards independence in pushing beyond rules. It sends the message that our intent is not to crush this independence, but to nurture its emergence. In whatever way possible punishment should be meaningful.

In some cases we need to distance our children from the context in which they have been misbehaving, while also trying to create a situation in which distancing is also a form of healing. In punishing our children we need to always keep in mind the fluid nature of their personality, which is still developing. The last thing that we want to do is create a fixation on the unresolved wounds and fears that led to misbehavior.

It is also vital that we are always conscious of the boundaries that delineate punishment that is healthy and constructive from that which is complicating and destructive. Imposing punishment in an authoritarian way, from above, for example by having the same set punishment for every "crime," or even for every time the same misbehavior repeats itself, may satisfy our desire for consistency and order. It may even work to the extent that it succeeds in eliminating unwanted behavior. Yet shocking a rat in a laboratory achieves the same effect. This kind of punishment is only effective on the outside. On the inside it is counterproductive, because the scars it creates mark off the pain and confusion that led to the misbehavior as a danger area, thus blocking insight and healing. Instead, by using misbehavior as an opportunity for dialogue and negotiation, for exploring the ethical implications of actions and the emotional charge they carry with them, acting out and subsequent discipline can become a catalyst that moves an adolescent towards maturity.

Moreover, in punishment as in everything else, teenagers see the significant adults in their life as models. Even their rebellion is part of a symbiotic relationship that is based on a very strong inner identification. Punishment provides an opportunity to learn. If teenagers perceive the adults in their life as imposing punishment that is designed to shrink and imprison the spirit, it will contribute to the creation of diseased souls. If punishment and what leads up to it involve creativity and are geared to produce insight and reflection, teenagers will take this example with them into their lives.

Never be Ashamed of Shame

We should continuously remind ourselves that the ultimate aim of any punishment response is to help create within our children's psyche the capacity for self-reflection and self-critique. This capacity is crucial if our children are to continue to learn and grow all through the course of their lives. They must be able assess what their boundaries are in every given situation, and must eventually learn to think clearly about the consequences of their actions for good and evil. Self-critique is a double-edged sword. The wrong kind of self-critique, harsh, repetitive and unyielding of insight, can paralyze and stifle energies and passions instead of liberating them.

Self-critique can lead to insight only if it is founded on a deeper layer of emotional openness, an ability to feel and even welcome the purging sting of shame. How often have we cringed at what we perceive as the shamelessness of our young people's behaviors and attitudes? Yet have we ever considered whether we have created a slot for their shame, a legitimate place within their psyche for shame to be expressed? Have we found the space within our discourse to share our own moments of shame when growing up?

In our staff training we have often repeated the idea that if the biblical prophets were alive today, they would compose elegies lamenting the disappearance from the world of the category of shame. If there were shame, there would be less reason for punishment, because shame is the most refined form of self-punishment. Overtly, it seems like shame has been excised from our lexicon of acceptable emotions, because it runs counter to the prevailing cultural demand that we accept ourselves, no matter who we are and what we have done. Subliminally, however, isn't it possible that it is the very brittleness of modern identity that has made the notion of shame almost taboo? The experience of shame has become obsolete within the anonymity of urban life that replaced the familiarity of the village and extended family. In front of whom are we to be ashamed in day to day life when intensive togetherness no longer exists?

One of the contributions of the Ethiopian children to Yemin Orde Youth Village has been their demonstration of the particular role that shame played in their cultural environment. When they detect a reason for shame, they cover their faces with both hands and produce a short sound of embarrassed laughter. Shame is a built-in human emotion; observe very young children encountering strangers and you will see them blush and hide behind their mother's skirt. By repressing it we block our access to 'dangerous' or humiliating memories. Hidden from our conscious minds, these lay embedded with a radioactive toxicity. Under these conditions, in the absence of shame and inner dialogue, paralyzing guilt can emerge to fuel irrational, acting-out behaviors and cause lasting damage to the personality.

In our Village our message is that shame is a legitimate emotion. We want the children to internalize an insight that they should carry with them through life - *one should never be ashamed of shame.*

Every year, we repeat the story of the King of the Khazars, who in early medieval times searched for the true religion, eventually engaging in a lengthy discussion of Judaism with a learned rabbi. At some point in their conversation the Khazar King confronted the rabbi with the incident of the golden calf, a biblical story that places the Jewish people, who the rabbi was defending, in a very bad light.

"You have shamed me, King of the Khazars," the rabbi says.

Emphatically, we drive home the association with

the story between royalty and shame: "A person who knows how to be ashamed is himself a king."

"To realize that you have committed wrongdoing or have experienced humiliation and yet not to be destroyed by that knowledge, that is greatness!" we say.

By associating the capacity to feel shame with the quality of greatness, shame's potentially corrosive influence on young egos is neutralized. The ability to reflect on painful memories without fear of drowning in humiliation opens the way for learning and growth and paves the way for meaningful inner dialogue. It also does something more: it allows psychic channels to childhood that may otherwise have been sealed to remain open and intact. Teenagers feel that they are what they have the potential to be, but they also know deep inside how small and powerless they are. All those things that cause them to be ashamed are thus repressed. When we teach adolescents to be able to say, "I was ashamed, and that's okay," then we have given them the vessels to deal with their weakness.

Equating shame with royalty is necessary because the legitimacy of shame has been so undermined by our culture. That is why instead of just conveying that "it's okay to be ashamed," we emphasize its connection with greatness, thus investing in the child's ego. The final product will be a quality of humility, the kind of humility that their personality, we believe, will be able to sustain even when they are in a leadership position, possess wealth or wield power. In the end, what is important is that the adolescent will not have to devote his or her future psychic energies to doing damage control on the experiences that he or she repressed as a child or teen. If a child failed, lied, broke, destroyed or stole, and we teach him that these things are wrong but don't allow space for shame, then he will lock these things away until they suddenly burst out some day, or sap his strength little by little like a hemorrhaging wound.

Instead, we can create a view of childhood, with all its humiliations, as a source of strength, and not a closed narrative that will take fifty years to open.

Sex and Violence

I will never forget Suzy, a startlingly beautiful young woman whose lovely exterior, of which she was well aware, hid a troubled inner world emanating from a tragic childhood. These two qualities made us even more anxious one night in August when she failed to return to the Village. The next day, as I was on the phone trying to get an update on her disappearance from the police, she appeared at my office door, her brown body covered only by a skimpy bathing suit and a towel. Behind her stood a bashful, muscular young man, 6'5" tall, as blonde as she was brown.

"I found him at the beach," she told me, "I'm going with him forever."

Relieved that she was alive, I also understood the whole story in a flash — an explosion of hormones!

"You're not going anywhere," I told her, "You're staying right here."

"It's my life," she said defiantly.

Meanwhile, outside my office, a group of young men and women had gathered, jealous and fascinated (a number of broken hearts among the men), and all fiercely attentive to the question of where this meeting was going.

Allen, the young man, was from a northern European country.

"What do you want from her?" I asked him.

His answer came in broken Hebrew but correct grammar, "I really love her."

From the tone of his voice and his seriousness, I understood that he had qualities that could not readily be seen as he stood in his wet, sandy bathing suit. My quick decision, to invite him to stay with us in the Village, proved to be the right one. Now, fifteen years later, reminiscing about that strange beginning of a wonderful union, Suzy can explicitly attribute her attraction to Allen to the kind of personality he was. He was out of the game of all the hunters who were after her as a conquest for status. During the 24 hours they spent together on the beach, it turns out that they were not indulging in orgiastic sex, but talking deeply about their respective families' stories and his search for his Jewish roots. They now have four children, a warm family life and an ongoing involvement in wider circles of caring and compassion.

The mistake in perception I committed when I initially presumed that Suzy and Allen's sexual attraction was devoid of a larger context is a common one. Most of the books and curriculum on sex education for adolescents concern themselves with specific, quasi-technical questions such as: "Under which circumstances should birth control be provided?" and "What we should tell our children about masturbation?"

Yet the extent to which teenage sexuality expresses complex social quotients, including the quality of the relationship between teenagers and adults, is largely ignored.

Far from being a function of raw animal desire, teenage sexual indulgence and promiscuity is greatly influenced by the search for social status. Often, the linkage between sex and status in the teenager universe mirrors their understanding of the world of adults. In the absence of a meaningful and multidimensional intergenerational dialogue with adults, adolescents will tend to grasp what is called the social weave as a well-policed but very shallow web. The "level" a person has reached on the social ladder is defined by his or her sexual partner, sexual visibility, and, in slightly different ways for young women or men, the extent of their sexual experience. When no alternative center of gravity has been created to anchor them in the past, future, earth and sky, adolescents often attempt to procure their identity using the coin of sexual experience.

This tendency is especially acute among teenagers growing up among adults who are not actively involved in creating community, adults who themselves live in a world where romantic and sexual attachments define social status and rank, and in which divorce is prevalent and the family a threatened institution. When adults look and act like teenagers, and lose their status as guide and mentor, then the world of the teenager unites with the world of the adult and the sexual mores of the adult world tend to penetrate into the teenage universe. The opposite is true as well; when a center of gravity that holds both the teenagers and their parents together in a single circle is created, the need to prove one's status through precocious sexual activity and conquest is diminished. Ultimately, the kind of emotional and intellectual dialogue that a young person develops with his or her lover will reflect the quality of the dialogue experienced with the adults in their life.

Much the same dynamic is at work where teenage violence is concerned. Teenage perpetrators of violent acts nearly always describe their motivation as survival, which in their world means the protection of their honor. The desire to live is what creates violence, because honor is survival, the sole and essential quality of their existence. Although to adults it might seem as if the increasingly violent world of teenagers makes no sense at all, for the teenagers, violence is almost always a response to a perceived defilement of honor. The desire to live is what creates the violence. Without the framework of the concentric circles and the horizontal and vertical lines, the inner point of honor has no context. When we are involved with past and future, and transcendence, then our honor is not so exposed and sensitive. Bereft of context, the sense of honor becomes an unguided missile. When we succeed in inculcating a sense of gravity and ballast secured by a broad context of emotional connections and intergenerational contacts, there is very rarely violence. This is true as much for schools as it is for individual families. Everyone is able to see things from the other side, to encircle each other, to trade points of view.

In Search of Lost Time

According to Donald Winnicott, a pediatrician who became, after Freud, one of the greatest of modern psychological theorists, mourning for the loss of childhood is a distinguishing characteristic of adolescence. In childhood, time has an infinite quality to it. A 20-minute recess can seem nearly endless, and the three months of a summer vacation feel like eternity. This almost dreamlike quality of time partly explains the capacity of children to become lost in a world of fantasy. But with the onset of adolescence comes a new sense of time. Time is marked by dramatic physical and emotional changes; it is no longer infinitely expansive. The journey to adulthood has begun.

Those teenagers whose childhood has been marred by trauma, abuse or deprivation enter adolescence with a feeling of loss, as if they have been robbed by fate of the paradisiacal time of childhood. Of course almost every child feels deprived in some sense; those who have siblings, for example, have had to compete for and share their parents' love, while those who don't have siblings feel deprived of siblings. And even for children who have lived exemplary "normal" lives, it is still undoubtedly difficult to adjust emotionally to the new sense of time that has imposed itself on their inner consciousness.

This is perhaps why so many teenagers have difficulty with the strict kind of schedule which the modern world and the modern education system imposes on them.

And this is why, in our Village, we try to be both firm and flexible in terms of time. We are firm in the sense that events – waking up in the morning, prayers, meals and classes – are all run according to a quite strict schedule. For example, I will never allow teens in the Village to see me walk in late for an event. In my estimation it is often better for me to miss a meeting altogether than to come late. I demand promptness from the rest of the Village staff, so that our teens can learn through personal example. We want teens to get used to the idea of exact times, because that is the way that the world they will eventually inhabits works. This is especially important because some of our youngsters, those from the Ethiopian immigrant community and from the Caucasus in the former Soviet Union, have grown up with parents from rural villages who have a completely different, and a much more fluid, conception of time. In pre-modern society sunrise, noon and sunset, the phases of the moon, and the seasons of the year measure time, not the abstraction of the clock. Part of full absorption into mainstream Israeli life is becoming familiar with exact notions of time.

While the Village and its staff run by the clock, we don't automatically expect the same from every youngster, and certainly not all at once. If children come from a place where discipline was not imposed, or from a place where too much discipline did not allow space to breathe, it is wrong to expect or enforce instantaneous change. At Yemin Orde we leave room for negotiation and dialogue so that our teenagers don't feel their inner sense of time trampled over by our demands. By allowing flexibility we offer some kind of compensation for the loss of childhood time. Alongside the abstract time represented by the clock, and without denying its importance, we try to consider inner time as it is experienced within each person. The framework of exact time must exist, both for the functioning of the institution and in order to create structures and boundaries. But by legitimating flexibility, by not insisting that each child follow a rigid schedule with total consistency, by allowing adolescents to flow between their own personal, inner sense of time and the demands of the institution – sometimes emphasizing temporal boundaries and sometimes relaxing them – time can stretch and the loss of childhood can be sweetened.

Let Them Sleep

What is true about class schedules is certainly valid in regards to sleep. Sleep is one of the most personal, inwardly directed activity we engage in. During sleep, the depth dimension of the psyche finds the time and space to express itself in dreams. The tumultuous psyche of the teenager needs sleep in order to work out the confusing changes he or she feels within them. Teenagers also use sleep as compensation, as comfort for pain or loss. One of the lessons I have learned about teenagers over the years is that sometimes you just have to let them sleep. Sleep can be like a cocoon in which a teenager wraps himself, only to emerge much later as a butterfly.

Earlier, I mentioned a teenager who came to live at Yemin Orde because his mother was in a mental hospital. We let this young man sleep almost to his heart's content, pretty much constantly for three years. Now he is blossoming. His psychic energies have been renewed, he is ready to face the world, and he is both self-confident and intellectually curious.

Which is not to say that in letting teenagers sleep you don't keep reminding them that they really should get up and participate in life. And sleeping too much can be a warning sign of involvement in drugs, that also needs to be examined. Even when we let children sleep, we do so after waking them, urging them to get up, and making a great show of defending the logic of the schedule. Our message is that the schedule is there, it is important, but we are not going to impose it by coercion. Discipline imposed solely by force will bring with it opposition, conflict and frustration, because it makes impossible demands. You can force things using punishment, by preventing pleasure and through other strategies. But then the basic experience will be of force, without any possibility of insight. This will stunt a teenager's development. We are willing to give a child time until he or she says, "Ok, I am ready." And, if you have faith in them, they eventually will be.

Parents and educators sometimes interpret a teenager's lethargy or desire to sleep as a form of rebellion. This is almost never the case. Once it has been established that their weariness is not drug-induced, we can assume that the teenage need for sleep stems from a lack of psychic energy, which they often feel as lack of physical energy. There is just too much going on within, too many contradictory external and internal demands. The system shuts down, retreats. The teenage appetite for sleep is often what psychologists might call "a regression in the service of the ego."

We have mentioned earlier that the teenage years are like another birth, another infancy. Teenagers sometimes have a deep desire to crawl back into the womb – under the covers, with the blanket pulled over their head. Even when it is necessary to push a teenager to get up on time, it is important to remember not to act as if their desire for sleep is a personal insult.

During the moratorium years of adolescence, we have to give a chance, as much as possible, for each teenager to create an order in their life that comes from them and that arises organically from within. This will not happen in a vacuum, simply by letting them alone. We need to present them with a schedule, with the idea of requirements and responsibilities. We need to have a continuous dialogue with them about being on time, about getting up in the morning, about sleep. But we must also avoid causing the scars that come from a relationship organized around the idea that our authority makes us strong, while their youth makes them weak. Teenagers should not get up in the morning simply from the power of threat. Although, as we have said, teenagers are resilient, they are also vulnerable. Defeating a teenager, inflicting negative blows, can cause damage that is difficult to repair. Although we may feel it is our task to make sure that the teenagers whose lives we are helping to guide gain the skills they need for survival and success, sometimes it really is better just to let them sleep.

Chapter Fourteen
A Mirror in the Sky

Sasha

When teenage lives are devoid of faith, attempts to find meaning in the face of their apathy and destructiveness are destined to failure. Unfortunately, too often the very mention of faith is immediately associated with organized religion and summarily rejected as a legitimate ingredient in the formation of our youngsters' emerging personalities. Adolescents deserve that the word "faith" be born anew for them, redeemed from the connotations and implications in which it has been imprisoned for so long, thus bestowing 'faith' with new youth.

Sasha, a teenager from Russia, taught me a lesson about the possibility of the rehabilitation of the word "faith." Sasha's exposure to the story of Abraham, considered in Judaism as the discoverer of monotheistic faith, was a terrible shock. Of all the stories he was introduced to at our Village, the Biblical story of the Binding of Isaac, in particular, gave him the chills.

"I never want to be part of a people whose founding father was willing to kill his son..." Sasha reacted contemptuously, dismissing with a single remark the option of embracing the people of the book and making their story part of his identity. In situations like this we try to remind ourselves to accept every reaction of a young person as a legitimate representation of his current emotional and cognitive state while understanding that further interpretations and responses will come in due time.

During the next three years Sasha had many opportunities to express his reservations or outright rejection of religious beliefs, often emphatically declaring himself an atheist. He openly flouted religious conventions and rituals by appearing in synagogue from time to time with his own anti-religious literature. In contrast to all his expectations he was not chastised, nor did we attempt to persuade him to change his beliefs.

The discussions we held were not geared towards anything resembling religious indoctrination, but instead underlined and flushed to the surface many of the fears and dilemmas he was struggling with in day-to-day life, so that they could be addressed legitimately. In spite of the transcendent center of the Torah dialogues, he gradually grasped their connection to real, earthy life.

The image of a father with a slaughtering knife at his son's neck is indeed a dreadful one. No wonder Sasha felt that that knife was also bent over his own neck. The story of Abraham and Isaac, and Sasha's reaction to it, reveals the nature of adolescence in spiritual search, which we rarely are able to recognize. Sasha's world was understandably shattered by the story of human sacrifice. The theme of intergenerational threat dramatically cut through to chaos at the heart of the adolescent's inner world, arousing memories of threats accumulated during years of viewing television and absorbing the narratives of violence so prevalent in contemporary reality and fantasy.

Yet Sasha's insistent rejection of the story paradoxically revealed a wish to engage in a search for his identity. Whenever we are confronted by assertions from our teenagers that sometimes seem like capricious rejections of our most cherished values, we need to have faith in our teenager's inner emotional logic, even when it is not as crystal-clear as it was in Sasha's case. These stances represent an attempt to engage in an ongoing, subterranean dialogue with us in which a transition from extreme to extreme may even stretch over the course of years. There is an inner dynamic to the provocations which youngsters repeatedly throw in our face that stems from their search for a separate identity.

Confronting these challenges to our values head-on creates a battleground on which we can never win. Instead we need to understand the spiral form in which insights are gained. It took Sasha three years to realize that the very story that provoked him so bitterly deserved a different interpretation. Sasha eventually concluded that the story of Abraham and Isaac in its wholeness is a repudiation of human sacrifice in a world in which it was a normative practice. The process which Sasha went through, which began with a convergence between his own raw and exposed emotional state and the harshness of some parts of the Biblical story, led eventually towards healing insights that were eventually be integrated into his spiritual world view and personality.

"There are no atheists in foxholes." In some ways, raising a teenager is like being in a foxhole. It is hard to survive the experience intact unless you have faith, and can convey this faith to your child. In Sasha's story, what enabled faith was not religious indoctrination but the opportunity, like Abraham, to experience shattering and despair in the face of an unacceptable reality, human sacrifice, and yet find himself ultimately able to raise the banner of the absolute value of all human life.

The kind of faith we need in order to raise children is not necessarily religious faith in the classic sense. Yet guiding our adolescents into adulthood is a spiritual task of the highest order that necessitates our identifying and drawing on the deep sources of our faith in life. The faith that we find within ourselves can be an opening through which we teach our adolescents about faith – faith in themselves, in life and in the existence of transcendent values and meaning. In this sense the transmission of faith is at the heart of the entire process through which an adolescent emerges into a whole adult.

Comfort Beyond Words in the Mystery of Life

For many centuries, the connection between education and spirituality was taken for granted. From the time when humans lived in hunter-gatherer tribes until the scientific enlightenment, maturation, in addition to the honing of survival skills, meant the absorption of spiritual knowledge and values. Adolescence was marked by a rite of passage in which each young person would have to demonstrate some kind of mastery of his or her culture's spiritual tradition. For some Native American tribes, for example, this rite was a vision quest, a physical and spiritual ordeal meant to culminate in a revelation. In the Jewish tradition the "bar mitzvah" celebrant, who has just reached adolescence, is meant to demonstrate familiarity with the Torah and the prayer services and to offer an original interpretation of a religious text. In various forms of Christianity catechism and confirmation ceremonies mark the period of coming of age.

For the past two hundred years much of the western world believed that scientific knowledge could replace religious truth in guiding humanity. Thus, just as adolescence began to emerge as a distinct period in which young people were meant to acquire the skills they need for adult life, western society, to a great extent, stopped thinking about the spiritual component in education. Now, in the post-modern age, we have painfully come to understand that science is a magnificent tool and an inspiring expression of the human spirit, but it is not going to solve all of humanity's problems. In fact, science's ability to shape and transform the natural and human environment may intensify some of these problems. After decades in which much of educational theory has purposefully ignored the question of spirituality, it is time to renew an ancient discussion whose focus is spiritual education. We cannot continue to rob our children of an essential part of their humanity: the capacity to feel holiness, to touch transcendent meaning. We do not necessarily need to make our teenagers religious, but we do have to acknowledge the facts of the human condition – that we need some kind of approach or relationship with the transcendent.

Transcendent Paralysis

And yet the transcendent can also be deeply problematic. Conceived in a one-dimensional way, the transcendent can paralyze and terrorize. Religious fundamentalism – whether Jewish, Christian or Islamic – in its efforts to separate believers from the "impurities" of the surrounding world, can create mental walls that lock our children into rigid and defensive patterns of thought, or cause them to abandon faith altogether. Our job as parents and educators is to try to open a path for our children towards faith and ideals that heal rather than hurt. How can we free religious education from the tendency to lock children into inflexible forms of faith that will either stifle them or that they will eventually reject? What kind of goals should we set for ourselves in the spiritual education of our teenagers? Although we at Yemin Orde are rooted in traditional Judaism, we hope our discussion will be just as relevant for members of other religious groups, as well as those whose faith cannot be defined in terms of any organized religion.

Teenagers need an anchor in a transcendent source of value and meaning in order to move with confidence towards the realization of their dreams. The anchors of past and future are necessary because our human identity is inextricably connected to memory and to our capacity to imagine and anticipate the future. But without an anchor in the transcendental, we would have no way to assess our lives, or put them into perspective. Like sailors in the open sea who depend on the North Star for navigation, only something that rises above them bright and steadfast can provide our teens with the immovable point of reference they need in order to make sense of their journey and their lives.

There is one great difference between the stars and the metaphysical heavens. The stars shine brightly, no matter what we think or do. But the "sky" that we are talking about, the top of the vertical line of our framework – the spiritual or transcendental anchor our teenagers need – reveals itself through the prism of our own subjectivity. In a certain sense the metaphysical sky is like a giant screen onto which the inner workings of our psyche are projected. This does not mean that the transcendent realm is only a projection of our thoughts and emotions, as some philosophers have proposed. But because we cannot fully grasp the infinite with our conscious, rational minds, any notion of it we may hold is tinged with the affect of our upbringing, our preconceptions, the stories we have been told and our own psychological state.

A Continuous Deepening Experience of the Infinite

Although the metaphysical sky described in our framework should provide an anchor for our teens, we by no means want them to see this sky as frozen and one-dimensional. Teens, who are still working to integrate the components of their personality into a stable identity, tend to think and experience life in a dualistic way. This dualism is often projected onto the heavens. The transcendent realm can come to represent terror and punishment, either by becoming the focus of irrational fears and superstitions or by casting a dark shadow of disapproval, and thus function as a soaring, concave mirror that reflects and amplifies already existing feelings of shame and guilt.

The teenage years, which are formative in so many ways, are often used by fundamentalist religious sects as a time of intense indoctrination. The adolescent tendency towards perceiving the world dualistically suits the fundamentalist agenda well; indoctrination, when it does not spark rebellion, works to fix the teenager's metaphysical conception at this point of rigidity and polarization, where the sky appears as static, inspiring obedience and fear.

Our ambition, to the contrary, is to begin a process of dialogue with the heavens that will continue for a teenager's entire life. Instead of "fixing" its nature in a rigid definition, we want our adolescents to have a continuously deepening experience of the infinite, of an absolute that is grasped in a multidimensional way.

Much of the rebellion against spirituality and religion that was characteristic of Western intellectuals in the 19th century and in the first part of the 20th century was caused by society's inability to educate towards a more complex and open conception of the divine. There is a Hasidic story about this set in the era in which enlightenment ideas were beginning to spread like wildfire through Eastern European Jewish communities. Exposed to the ideas of scientific rationalism, one young man found it impossible to believe anymore in the concept of God he had formulated as a child – as an awesome being with a long white beard sitting on a royal throne. Troubled, he went to ask a Hasidic Rebbe, or spiritual master, for advice. The Rebbe, intuiting the young man's state of mind, greeted him with the words: "The God you no longer believe in I don't believe in either."

How are we to guide our teens towards an open-ended relationship with the transcendent, one that will continue to develop and grow? First of all, as in other areas we have discussed, we have to try to remove the aspect of threat that can darken the sky for our teenagers. Teens can perceive fate as an irrational and demonic presence in their lives, and parents and teachers, if they are not mindful, can give power to this feeling. Sentences like, "If you don't watch out, you are going to end up like so and so," and talk about divine punishment or vengeance in general, even when it is not directed towards your child, can enhance teenagers' sense of irrational powers.

So can anxiety about religious observance; non-verbal or even subconscious feelings that parents or teachers convey that make a teenager feel that something terrible might happen if a particular ritual is not completed, a belief is questioned or a taboo is broken. Our goal is for the sky to shine; we want this radiance to accompany our children and give them strength throughout their long journey in life. For this to happen we don't have to speak necessarily about love. It is enough to remove the atmosphere of fear and threat that often sneaks in as we attempt to teach our children about transcendent notions of right and wrong. Removing threat from teenage lives is already a potent act of love. Love-talk can raise expectations that cannot be fully realized. When threat is removed, the pool of love will fill up from underground sources.

Targeting God

By avoiding the anxiety that can accompany religious education, in fact by not talking much about God at all, we can avoid making the transcendent a target for rebellion. The adolescent, in search of self-definition, is always looking for such targets. Those of us who are part of a particular religious tradition or cherish specific beliefs wish to transmit these beliefs to our children. But if a teenager senses that this transmission is freighted with concern and anxiety, if religious teachings are accompanied by an open or subliminal threat to withhold love or support from a child who rejects these beliefs, it is as if a gilded invitation to rebel has been extended.

The potential tragedy in this set of circumstances is that rebellion means polarization; once again, God is "set up" to represent one side of the duality that exists within the teenage psyche, thus "freezing" God and blocking spiritual development. Our hope is that our teenagers will come to experience God as a totality. Just as we hope to create a sense of continuity and internal unity in the flow of time from past to future represented by the horizontal line, so, too, we wish to allow our children to experience the transcendent as a place or entity beyond time in which all the fragments of their inner and outer world merge into oneness.

But how can faith be taught without focusing on or "targeting God?" If our children realize how important it is to us that they have faith, they will rebel. And yet is not any faith of utmost importance? How can we escape this quandary?

Perhaps, most importantly, we must learn to demonstrate faith rather than demanding it. The most effective way for our teens to learn about faith is by feeling the faith we have in them. We can think about it as we do a geometrical theorem in which the angles of two sides of a triangle define the angle of the third side. If we have faith in our children, and they see that we also have faith in God, they will absorb the lesson of faith in God even if it is not explicit. We need to have faith in our children's goodness, in their abilities, in their ultimate success in life. They will understand the profound inner connection between our faith in God, our faith in life, and our faith in them, and will eventually follow the stream of faith back to its source.

This won't necessarily happen instantly, although

sometimes it does. We have to be ready, though, to have faith in our child's religious development as we would in a barren field that we have just begun to seed. It is even possible that our child's religious faith will awaken only when we are no longer an immediate presence in their life – in missing us, for instance, the faith that we represent will become available to them. Sometimes this process takes more than one generation, and in the end, it is our grandchildren who will ultimately inherit our faith, as they hear about us from their parents, and sense the wholeness of our personality unimpeded by the negative interactions that sometimes mar relations with parents.

In terms of transmitting faith, as in other matters, parenting should be understood as an act of *Tikkun Olam,* whose ripples reach the broadest circles of our human affiliation, not an expression of our need to allay our existential insecurity by replicating ourselves. Appreciation for other religious traditions and the idea that there is a quality of religiosity that transcends every specific expression of faith is an integral part of the children's experience in our Village.

It was only natural, therefore, that our dialogue with Tibetan educators led us to invite Tibetan teenagers from the Tibetan Children's Villages in India and Nepal for an extended stay in Yemin Orde. When the Tibetan teenagers came to our Sabbath prayer service and meditated as we chanted and read the Torah, we saw this as part and parcel of fostering our own spiritual development.

When I finally reached Dennis, a child of Muslim and Christian lineage living on the streets of war-torn Sarajevo, what we talked about was his dream of a life in Israel.

"You can rest easy," I told him before hanging up the phone. "As far as I'm concerned, you can consider your Israel dream already fulfilled."

From the moment I first greeted him at the airport until his graduation ceremony several years later, Dennis's unique ethnic and religious background silently played a significant role, becoming an asset and providing the glue that cemented together disparate experiences and parts of his personality. Dennis eventually returned to build his life in Europe, and remained true to himself and his own original roots. His presence and the presence of others like him in our Village has made me feel that we are fulfilling, in our own small way, the Biblical promise, "My house will be called a house of prayer for all peoples."

We don't want to mark God for rebellion by focusing on obedience, retribution, or even love. We do, however, want to help open the channels through which our children can be guided on their journey by a living connection with the metaphysical sky above. The vector pointing upwards should rise towards a horizon in which all the fragments of a sometimes shattered existence merge into a unified whole. If we can see totality and wholeness outside ourselves, at the point at which existence transcends our grasp, we will gain the ability to feel the inner unity of our own psyche and identity.

Our ability to grasp ourselves as whole emanates from our ability to see the whole outside of ourselves. This is what we wish for our children; that the sky above them, the beyond which surrounds and envelops their lives, should be experienced as a place where the pieces of life's puzzle, the seeming contradictions and conflicts, coexist in harmony. Then, as the Psalmist says, "Like an infant at his mother's breast," the act of turning towards the sky will become a moment of profound solace and comfort.

Chapter Fifteen

Anchors in the Past

Gideon

Gideon remembered his father, Prosper, a police officer, as a man whose bearing and manners expressed the epitome of self-confidence and who was loved and admired by the community he served. He was everything a child might dream of in a father; a hero in the street and a warm and loving parent and husband at home. Despite all the pressures and emergencies that went with his job, Gideon recalls how his father always seemed to be there at bedtime, to tell stories and tuck him in.

"How did he manage to be there for us?" Gideon, who now has his own children and a busy career, sometimes marvels.

Gideon's idyllic childhood didn't last forever. Gradually, his father's behavior changed, and so did his personality. Rumors that Officer Prosper was on the take had begun to spread in the community. He began to withdraw emotionally, and his mood swung from brooding melancholy to angry outbursts. By the time the reports reached the local newspaper, Prosper could no longer bear the shame. He was found in a nearby orchard, a self-inflicted bullet wound in his head.

After his death, the family broke apart. Gideon, age 13, was sent to our Village. The crisis his family had endured and the shock of the abrupt loss of the home he had grown up in was evident in his appearance, but so was the strength and stamina he radiated. His anger towards his father was at the center of his emotional vocabulary during his sessions with therapists and counselors. Yet hanging over his bed, concealed behind a larger photo of a giraffe on the African Savannah that could be flipped up, was a passport photo of his father in uniform, which he had marked with a thick black margin.

In a recent deep into-the-night conversation I had with Gideon, he talked about the some of the insight he had gained in the process he went through after losing his own father.

"In a sense my father abandoned me, too," Gideon said, "but somehow I was able to keep him alive with me, despite my anger.

"I remember," he continued, "the stories you made me tell in the dining hall during Saturday dinners – the same ones that my father told me. When I ran out of good stories from my father, I used to go to the library, read storybooks, and tell them to the others as if he had told me those stories as well. And then, when I was fifteen, I recall stepping out of your office, after one of those conversations, with a clear direction. The day will come, I told myself, when I will sit at my father's desk, in a uniform just like the one he wore in the photo I had hung, and the community which had humiliated him would know: 'This is Prosper's son.'"

This dream was the glue that helped him rebuild his life. The bright past living on through the stories he had heard in childhood, and the aspiration, rooted in this past, to do honor to his father's name, formed a pathway through the turbulent and agonizing present that allowed Gideon to unify his memories of the past with his goal for the future. The Village worked consistently with him in order to make this occur, and there were ups and downs on the way. Yet once Gideon graduated from high school and maneuvered his way into the army as a cadet in the military police, rising quickly in the ranks with much encouragement from us, we knew that his father's desk was within his reach.

Time as an Uninterrupted Flow

Gideon's story is not uncommon in Yemin Orde Youth Village – a childhood suddenly interrupted by events and forces that children cannot fully comprehend and which are beyond their control, which break the normal trajectory of their life and creates new and terrifying circumstances. Our aim in Gideon's case was to ensure that the tragic events and injuries inflicted on his young life would not create an irreparable fissure in his inner experience. This would have damaged his chances to ultimately create a unified identity in which the present draws coping energies from the past, which forms a vision, even a vague one, of the future.

A defined and unified identity provides us with the inner strength to continue our journey into the unknown and yet remain ourselves. Endurance in time is perhaps the most basic raw material from which identity is formed. The notion of identity is anchored in the feeling that, despite my changing circumstances, something essential about me remains the same. Without memory, the past that lives on in the present, we would lose our sense of identity, as amnesiacs do. We would forget who we are. If we experience time flowing from past to the future in a broad, uninterrupted stream, it means that our identity is stable. This stability gives us the confidence to believe in ourselves, to explore life and to run the gauntlet of its challenges. This model of identity, one that rests on solid ground yet is continuously graced with a dynamic element, is the kind of identity to which teenagers ultimately aspire.

But for the adolescent just emerging from childhood, achieving this kind of unified identity is a lengthy and painful process, and one that can seem, from his perspective, hopeless. In the training sessions for our new youth counselors we compare the adolescent psyche to a *Tel*, a biblical Hebrew term that describes a hill where successive civilizations have built cities, and the archeological ruins of each layer in time jut jaggedly into the previous layer. On the top of the Tel there may be a thin layer of earth, adorned by tall grass and lush flowers in the springtime. But beneath the grass and the flowers are the stones of collapsed houses, scraps of pottery and fragments of assorted tools, whose origins must be sorted out by archeologists whose training and knowledge of historical artifacts prepares them for the painstaking work of assembling these puzzles.

It is difficult, especially when confronting enraging behaviors, to remember that although adolescents may put on a good show of self-confidence, beneath the surface of their psyche are the jumbled experiences of childhood which have not yet been assembled within the context of a stable identity. The basic experience of subjective time as an uninterrupted flow is ruptured by emotions that the adolescent may not have the vessels to contain, by memories he or she cannot integrate, or by a numbness that stems from withdrawal from the task of comprehending a painful and complicated world. Experience has taught us that only an adult that has cultivated an inner conviction that the fragments do indeed all fit together, that what we are looking at are pieces of a puzzle and not a random heap of debris, will be able to significantly help in the work of integration. If we can keep in mind both the child and the adult, both the past and the future, when looking at our adolescents, we can help create within them an inner space where the fragments can be assembled into a unified personality.

The Unfinished Business of Childhood

At the onset of adolescence the pain of the bruises acquired in childhood rises to the surface, flooding consciousness with their power. Adolescence is, as we have mentioned, a kind of rebirth or recreation. Just as in the Biblical account of the process of creation, "The earth was chaotic and unformed, and darkness covered the surface of the deep," so, too, in the recreation that is adolescence. Rebirth springs out of darkness and chaos and rubble from the unchartered depths.

Even a so-called "normal" childhood is filled with trauma. Parents quarrel and show it in one way or another, and no matter how hard we try to hide the harshness that sometimes shadows the most loving relationships, children always know. All couples pass through problems at work, emotional disappointments, the illness and death of relatives and parents. Children absorb it all. Who utterly escapes the pain and sadness that sometimes overwhelm all else in the real world? Children feel whatever is going on in the adult universe, whether inside the family or outside on the street. Although children seem to live in a world of their own, it is a world that needs protection, love and attention from the parallel universe of the adults. When clouds block the sun in the world of adults, the children's universe is also darkened. This darkness can stunt a child's emotional growth, and thus leave indelible marks on their soul.

There is the potential for much suffering within the world of the children as well. Siblings compete for attention and love, hurting each other in the process. Classmates insult, manipulate and reject each other during the course of the years in elementary school. Children are singled out for ridicule – because they are too fat, too short or have a learning disability. Some suffer physical abuse at the hands of their schoolmates or neighborhood toughs. Even some of the bullies suffer from the shame and guilt of knowing they have caused pain.

Then there are the "little" wounds. A two-year old falls and bruises his knee, and no one is there to hug him and to explain to him that the world will soon be right. A four-year old is lost in a department store for twenty minutes and feels, suddenly, the terror of abandonment. There is the everyday suffering that comes from living in a world not designed for children. Children are often forced to adjust to the urgencies of the adult world as they are dragged from bed, hurriedly dressed and fed, and rushed to school so parents can get to work. In the past few decades children have been confined, in many places, to smaller and smaller spaces, and prevented from wandering freely through our neighborhoods, as many of us did as children, because the streets have become too dangerous and unpredictable. One wound opens another.

Why do the painful parts of childhood become reactivated at adolescence? One way to look at it is that people are instinctually led to at least try to resolve the basic issues of one stage in life before moving on to the next stage. All unfinished business must achieve some kind of closure. Their Tel must be excavated. Everything that went on in childhood is part of the material from which teens must forge an identity – and identity, defining who I am, to myself and others, is perhaps the central issue of adolescence. Nothing that is pertinent to that question can really be swept under the rug for long.

The Healing Power of Adolescence

The reactivation of the unfinished business of childhood is not necessarily a bad thing. Instead, we can view adolescence as an hour of grace, an opportunity and a blessing, because adolescents possess an abundant store of the quality of resilience. The mysterious energy that powers the enormous transformations that characterize adolescence also contains healing powers.

One of the remarkable aspects of life in our Village is that there are so many opportunities to witness these powers of resilience and healing. The traumas that are common to many of our Village's children often do not have their first cause within the small circle of family. Frequently, it is the cruel nature of the world we are living in that has disrupted the life of the family, forced the children into seeking refuge outside their home, and stripped away the social environment from which the family drew its identity, causing death, exile and separation. For children who have experienced such losses and traumas reality sometimes feels like a walk through two distorting mirrors that are facing and reflecting each other – creating a maze of confusing emotions and images. A child may feel doubly cursed, once by the hurt and loss normal to childhood and internal family dynamics, and, secondly, by being from a foreign culture or a marginal social class.

Lily

Lily arrived in Israel after a nightmarish journey that lasted far longer than she ever thought it would. Her hardships were not over; when she descended from the plane, she expected her distant relatives to meet her at the airport and take her to their home. A journalist found her hours later sitting on her luggage and weeping.

We learned about her from the weekend edition of the paper, and offered to bring her to Yemin Orde. For us, Lily's story has become synonymous with the way in which parental absence can create not only a vacuum, but a cavity filled with the pus of concentrated human evil.

Lily's story begins in a Muslim Middle Eastern country, with parents who were never well-suited for each other, not least because her father was many decades older than her mother.

Lily's mother escaped from her mismatched marriage, threw away the veil she had been required to wear over her face, and reached Europe where she started over again with a new man her own age. Lily's father also left home and disappeared into the mountains. At the age of 14, Lily, disguised as an Islamic nomad from one of the indigenous tribes in the area, made her way to the Turkish border. When she crossed over the border at night, she thought her troubles were finally over, but she was wrong. With no passport or identifying documentation Lily was cast immediately into prison, and in the feminine version of Midnight Express, was horrendously abused first by the police patrol who arrested her and again later by prison guards.

Lily's resourcefulness in jail eventually paid off. She managed to make contact with the Israeli consul in Istanbul, and remembering the exact names and addresses of her relatives in Israel, convinced him to work for her release. From then on her path to the airport was clear.

When Lily arrived in our Village, she was emotionally devastated. Her emotional deficits and lack of an inner sense of security and trust in humankind stretched back to her early childhood. The only thing she had going for her, it seemed, was survival instincts and a strong desire to live. This is what had brought her to Israel. Lily was a loner, by dint of the circumstances of her life; her absorption into the life of the Village through friendships with other children was not easy. As with every child opening a new chapter in their life after trauma, disappointment and wandering, the first stage may seem to involve little more than enjoying the security of food and shelter. Yet we have seen over and over again how crucial this period is in the long term. In Lily's case, as in other cases, all her finely honed survival instincts were attuned to the task of reflecting on the nature of the place in which she had arrived, and puzzling out her conclusions.

Almost as a form of conscious experimentation, Lily produced a battery of "tests" to see how we would respond: sarcastic remarks, curses and vulgar language, direct disobedience of our rules, violence and disappearances.

Sometimes I wondered how teens such as Lily are able to create such a sophisticated plan to challenge and explore the crucial question: Who is the adult who is standing in front of them, claiming the role of guidance in their lives? This is where the concept of "plan" versus "plan" effectively comes into play.

Lily began to settle down as she subliminally sensed that we also had a plan. Our plan was not a syllabus, nor a curriculum, nor a book of rules, nor a list of skills she had to acquire. Instead, our plan was an inner outline meant to form a positive mirror image naturally corresponding to the chaotic "plan" that her bitter experiences had produced. In her acting out Lily was showing us that the wounds she had suffered had created within her a fragmented consciousness where the past was cordoned off by boundaries of pain, the future obscured in clouds of fear, and her connection to others blocked by layers of mistrust.

Our work was to show her that we saw her as a whole person, with a past that could be salvaged as meaningful even with its pain, a future that we had faith in, and potential we would help cultivate. The vibrancy of life in Yemin Orde where she now found herself, in a completely natural way, began to wear down her harsh reactions to human contact. The lines and circles conveyed by the contents of all our encounters with Lily first manifested in soft pastel colors in the background, and gradually began to emerge sharp and luminous. As Lily began to detect the contours of our "plan" – past, future, earth, sky, and the circles of *Tikkun* – she began to feel more rooted in the existential present and the furious pendulum swings of her behavior began to calm. It took three years until Lily's core of purity and basic human goodness recharged to the point that it could serve as the center of gravity of her emerging adult identity.

Years later, when I occasionally meet Lily and

others who arrived in our Village in similarly devastated conditions, they often ask me, "How were you able to stand me?"

What I feel they are really saying, with an almost indiscernible wink, is, "You passed my test. Cheers!"

A Sensation of Inner Time

As Gideon's and Lily's stories show, when we create the right conditions, the powers of healing which the adolescent psyche possesses in abundance can do their work. We need to help teenagers feel time as an uninterrupted flow, and feel the connection between their past, present and future. And we can do this by causing our teenagers to feel the past come to life in the present.

Without prying or insisting, and without taking on the role of psychotherapists, we have to send the message to our teens that they can talk about their open wounds – the gaping holes, pain and uncertainty whose origin reaches into their childhood. Although we keep reminding ourselves that our children are suffused with words, and the bridge to children is not through words but rather through our own inner transformation in relation to them, the power of speech in this aspect of the work of healing cannot be denied. Through language, past events can be brought to life and consciousness. We have to encourage and legitimate the verbalization of past experiences. By creating an atmosphere in which aspects of the past can be legitimately remembered and discussed, we conjure within the child a sensation of inner time, time that includes memory and is not confined and delineated by the stimuli of the moment. The child senses the depth-dimension within the vessel of consciousness, where healing can take place and from which, as in the case of Gideon, he or she can move forward.

The kind of discourse that has enabled the

adolescents in Yemin Orde Youth Village throughout the years to verbalize pain from the past does not need to take place only in focused and self-conscious bursts of attention, as in therapy. Instead, we try to touch upon the past on many different occasions, as part of a continuing conversation with each adolescent. One way to demonstrate the legitimacy of reflecting on childhood is by referring to one's own childhood. Talking about the pain as well as the joy that you experienced in childhood will create a reality in which articulating memory is acceptable and even encouraged.

The challenge, for both teachers and parents, is to create intimacy and reveal personal pain rooted in the past without negatively affecting one's moral or emotional authority. This always takes a certain degree of good judgment. We have to be able to offer personal revelations to our teenagers that will signal the legitimacy of touching childhood pain. But we need to carefully select and express these revelations using the healthy part of our psyche. Ideally, our adolescents need to see us leading the way in exploring complicated feelings from the past, but they don't need to necessarily see us in pain right now. It might be wise to choose to reveal childhood vulnerabilities that have already been resolved, not those that are still gaping wounds.

If we open the path for our teenagers we will see – almost magically, gently and slowly, right before our eyes – the broken shards of the Tel gathered up. This is not just a utopian vision. An inner time flow is created. Incidents from long ago are seen as alive and available for reshaping through external dialogue and internal reflection and the parts of experience which were cut off, kept isolated and apart, are magnetized. Pieces come together. Gaps are overcome. A sense of the unity of the personality overcomes feelings of detachment and incoherence.

Making the Past Alive in the Present

The past can become present in public as well as private conversations. In A.S. Neill's experimental school Summerhill children's assemblies were an important component of their community. Imitating in a way the historical Greek Polis, where democracy was born, the focus was on airing and finally voting on regulations, issues and disputes relevant to the day-to-day life in the school. In Yemin Orde our regular assemblies and group discussions always try to touch on some aspect of our teenagers' past, creating an atmosphere in which the past is neither ignored nor denied. Sometimes, discussions of current events in the collective life of the Village spur children to express traumas from the past, while others listen attentively.

Recently, the highway and road authorities constructed new signs on the highway and road leading upwards to Yemin Orde. Strangely, these new signs, which indicated the direction to other nearby villages, simply ignored our existence. The youngsters found the old signs, which included direction to our Village, in a ditch on the side of the road. The discussion that week was heated.

"How dare they wipe us from the map of Israel?" some of them shouted.

Although I was angry with the authorities and could think of no logical explanation for what they had done, I was grateful for this wonderful therapeutic gift. The feeling that our Village had suddenly become an abused underdog, ignored and insulted by forces stronger than us, evoked wellsprings of concealed pieces of the children's narrative that might have taken hundreds of hours of therapy to emerge.

Individually, I make a practice of keeping doors to the past open by asking each youth about his or her family and schools attended before reaching us. I might ask a youngster about memories from his or her country of origin

— about spring in an Ethiopian village or Russian children's songs.

Once, in northern India, talking to children of the Tibetan Children's Village who had left their ancestral homeland, I made a point of asking what they missed most about home.

"Yak meat, the way our mothers knew how to prepare it," was the common answer. The Tibetan officials later told me that they did not approve of the question I had asked.

"What use is it to awaken feelings of nostalgia and longing among the children?" they suggested. "We can't get yak meat down here in India. We can't give them home cooked food."

I disagreed. "You must let the children articulate their longing," I told them, "or it will gnaw at them from within."

Even feelings of failure can be reinterpreted through dialogue. I'll never forget a young woman named Adina who had no father, a mother who was barely functional and a grandfather who was constantly in some form of legal or financial trouble. From which parental figure was Adina to draw strength in shaping her identity? It seemed to me that her grandfather was the best bet. I encouraged Adina to talk about him, by asking about him each time we met, and made sure that I was not judgmental in my reactions. Gradually, Adina allowed herself to shape a new interpretation of her grandfather's adventures. She began to see her grandfather as a "rascal" rather than a criminal, for which we had no proof what he really was. She now included in her view of her grandfather the idea that he was someone who had an irrepressible love of life, echoing her own verve that kept getting him into trouble but also allowed him to bounce back again.

This reinterpretation of her grandfather's behavior

allowed her to release her own powers of resilience and love of life. She was no longer as embarrassed by her grandfather. She could claim him as her own, not as an ideal model for life, but as a precursor passing along a fundamental vitality and passion that Adina could channel in her own directions.

This definite achievement was not only the result of an isolated series of verbal interactions, but part of a context in which dwelling on the past is normal. We can reinforce this sense of shared fate in many different ways. We can bring our own parents more actively into the lives of our children. We can hang up photographs of ancestors on the walls of our living room. We can reminisce with our children about the events we have passed through as a family, and encourage them to talk about their memories. Again, we do not need to be aggressive in examining the past. We are not trying to do psychotherapy. We are trying to make the past alive in the present, and thus susceptible to interpretation; to the gentle light of the mind, to the healing powers the teenager himself possesses.

Casting Anchors in the Past

At times it is desperately painful to live up to the golden rules you have set for yourself in raising adolescents. We at Yemin Orde have always maintained that an adolescent's awareness and identification with his or her ancestral past is a crucial component in constructing an emerging identity. This principle is for us unequivocally clear. In normal circumstances it is not difficult to provide the connections and content that will enhance and strengthen this fundamental awareness. Yet its determinate importance in a youngster's life means that even in circumstances that are difficult, we have to go the extra mile in order to provide our teenagers with essential links to their collective past. The very effort to find value in the story that is available, even when one has to engage potentially toxic narratives, can itself be perceived by adolescents as an affirmation of their identity.

Chapter Sixteen

Narratives to Live By

Desta

When a highly respected Ethiopian elder was accused of molesting a very young Ethiopian girl, his grandson at Yemin Orde experienced the accusation as a mortal attack on his own honor and integrity, and perhaps even on his very right to live. At a funeral for a family member, which I attended with him, Desta told me, "The next grave will be mine," implying that his grandfather's arrest was evoking in him suicidal thoughts. I hugged him and promised him that he was not alone in this, while asking myself, "How on earth will I be able to show that my promise extends beyond verbal sympathy?"

The newspapers' coverage of the arrest and prospective trial – complete with an illustration of a young girl fearfully gripping a teddy bear and overshadowed by an elderly man – made me feel even more despairing. I was certain that the police authorities would not have pursued this case without solid evidence. The weekend editions of the tabloid papers expanded on the story and began to implicate the entire Ethiopian culture as the background for these lurid events. They claimed that a kind of duplicity existed within Ethiopian culture that tolerated sexual crimes under the protective aura of respectability. The newspapers meant to demythologize the Ethiopians, who until now had largely been seen as throwbacks to Biblical times in their innocence and purity. As if this case had released a genie from its bottle, prejudices and fears about the exotic, other than what until now had been repressed, began to emerge.

For thousands of Ethiopian Jews, who for centuries had seen their elders as the ultimate embodiment of their culture's wisdom and values, the media reports induced a state of hurt and numbness. The result for the Ethiopian youngsters in our Village was a kind of confusion that adversely affected their ability to function and do their schoolwork. This reaffirmed for me the power of ancestors, as represented by the elderly, to have a tangible and immediate affect on teenage lives, for good or bad.

But for Desta the issue was one of life and death. We decided that we had to show Desta and the other Ethiopians in our Village that we really stood with them, and with their culture. We decided to form a fund that would combat the negative publicity in the media that was in the process of creating a noxious association between Ethiopian culture and sexual misbehavior. This dovetailed with another principal we held dear, namely, that education worth its name must attempt to take a shaping part in the public discourse of a society. This existential quality, more than anything else, is what transforms an institution from simply being a warehouse for children – which in the best case provides maintenance and processing – into a true educational entity.

The lawyers demanded that experts in Ethiopian culture be allowed to testify as witnesses for the defendant, in order to unravel what exactly did happen between the elderly man and the young girl. In that way we wished to legitimate Ethiopian culture as a crucial nexus from which understanding and judgment about the truth of events could emerge, thus placing it on par with Western observation and judgment. Our law team vigorously protested prejudicial statements by the Tel Aviv District Court judge implying that Ethiopian society was primitive, as well as the judge's allusions that sexual abuse was rampant within the culture. By enlisting our Village and members of the larger Ethiopian community in a battle for the honor of their heritage, we let them know that they were not alone and at the same time helped them activate their own powers of resistance to the dismantling of their pride in the past.

The lawyers hired by Yemin Orde took the case to the Israeli Supreme Court, arguing that the District Court had been stained by prejudice. In several important newspapers the focus of the coverage of the trial changed, as journalists started questioning the stereotypes that the court had disseminated. Everyone in the Village was kept informed and involved throughout the course of the trial.

Wholeness is Hidden Within the Fragmentary

Our intention was not to "clear" the elder of charges that may or may not have been true, but rather to ensure that the justice system and media not be allowed to pronounce a verdict on all of Ethiopian culture, and thus rob the younger generation of a major component of their identity. The idea that every young person has the right to be meaningfully connected to their ancestry commits us to sometimes going very far in sending the message that the disunited and confusion of the present does not corrode our ability to see wholeness and value imbedded in the past.

By having faith in the value of the past we believe that the potential for wholeness lies hidden within the fragmentary, and can be reconstituted through the active mediation of human will and effort. To set anchors in the past it is often just as important to engage in a process of facing and clarifying even the darker corners associated with one's older generation. As we do this we sometimes have the opportunity to widen the circle, to understand the broader context from which our ancestors emerge and to know that no Pandora's boxes remain whose contents we have ignored.

Desta, I am happy to report, received rabbinic ordination and a degree in education. Married and the father of four children, he is now a highly respected teacher at the Yemin Orde high school.

Living Waters from Wellsprings of Identity

Through the years we have learned how the sense of time as an uninterrupted flow, which is essential for the formation of a healthy personality, must stretch beyond personal time. The collective past of the group into which a child is born is as inherently significant to the child as his or her own personal history. What our teenager is trying to forge is not only an inner identity, but also a social identity. A major part of an adolescent's aim is to locate his or herself within the social milieu, both in the boundaries of a peer group and within the culture as a whole. They intuit, as well, that success in the future is dependent on social identity. Although it would be a better world if everyone, no matter the family or ethnic group, had the same opportunities and the same challenges, teenagers know that this is not the case. Within a child's psyche the culture and history into which he or she was born can be as significant as their personal experiences during childhood. Teenagers should feel empowered to explore and interpret the meaning of their cultural background, so that it is free of negative and confining stereotypes.

The amazing capacity of children and teenagers to see themselves as part of something larger than themselves, and to use this larger identity as material with which to build their life, again and again surprises us. We have been privileged to witness this process many times in the context of the Jewish return to Zion from their various far-flung Diaspora.

Over the past fifteen years the mass immigration to Israel has brought hundreds of thousands of Jews from the former Soviet Union, where Communist authorities systematically erased Jewish identity. Hundreds of teenagers from the former Soviet Union have made their way to our Village during this period. Some of their stories provide extraordinary examples of the way in which a teenager can use fragments of information from an ancestor's life to build a new identity.

Tanya

Take the story of Tanya, who grew up as a Provo-Slavic Christian in a small town in the Ukraine. One Sunday, Tanya was sitting with her grandfather in church, when he suddenly he leaned over to whisper in her ear that he wanted to speak to her outside.

He said, "As a teenager I was forced into a crowded railway car used for transporting cattle. My family was there, and so were most of the town's Jews. The end of the line was one of the death camps we heard about through rumors. For two days and two nights we rode in the sealed car, the stench of human waste in the stale air becoming unbearable. On the third day I decided that I would try to escape. As the train slowed down I squeezed through a crack in the side of the car I was in and jumped! I was terrified of getting caught. I hid in a barn. The barn stood right here, where the church now stands. I was convinced that if any of the Ukranians found me, they would immediately turn me in to the authorities. But – I *was* found by a Ukranian family, who adopted me instead of turning me in. A few years later I married one of their daughters – your grandmother."

"Why are you telling me this?" Tanya asked.

"Because of your voice," her grandfather responded. "Now that you've grown up, your voice reminds me so much of mother's voice that I had to tell you."

Her grandfather's story changed Tanya's life. She

read everything she could get her hands on about Israel and Judaism. Eventually she brought her grandfather to the Israeli consulate in Kiev, where he proved he was Jewish by reciting the *Shema Yisrael* – one of the prayers he remembered from childhood. Tanya's Jewish ancestry was recognized and she became eligible to emigrate to Israel, where she ended up at Yemin Orde.

If Tanya had heard this story as a young child or as a grown woman, chances are that it would not have changed her life. But the teenage years are years of transformation and have enormous power to rejuvenate identity. A sliver of a story, but as long as that sliver hints towards a whole world, it can have tremendous potency in the eyes of a teenager.

Hidden Qualities

Another young Ukranian who found his way to Yemin Orde knew only one thing about his Jewishness. He knew his grandfather had come from a small town called Uman, "a backwaters that nobody has ever heard of," in his grandfather's words. I told this young man that Uman is now the most celebrated town in the Ukraine because it is the place where Rebbe Nachman of Braslav, one of the deepest and most beloved of Hasidic masters, chose to live during the last years of his life, and to be buried upon his death.

When talking to Yemin Orde youth, I often refer to Reb Nachman's famous sayings and songs, such as, "Life is a very narrow bridge and the most important thing is not to fear at all," although I add a stanza, alluding to the youngsters' newly found home, in which the bridge widens and there is no reason to fear at all.

During the years of Soviet rule the town of Uman was inaccessible. But now Reb Nachman's gravesite has become the site of a pilgrimage that attracts thousands of visitors each year to the town.

"Can you imagine; your great-great grandfather must have been a disciple of Rebbe Nachman?" I have said to this boy on numerous occasions, including when repeating a teaching of Reb Nachman's to the whole school. That one word, "Uman," has become the source from which this young man's entire identity can spring, a source that connects him to Israeli society and to an entire spiritual legacy. The point is not about Jewish identity, but rather the centrality of the teenage search for identity as a whole.

For a number of years now we have been joined in our Village every summer by a group of inner-city youth from Baltimore, most of them African-Americans. I am always struck by the extent to which their exposure to the ancestry stories told to them by our Ethiopian, Russian and South American youngsters moves them. They find themselves relating to their own ancestral stories within a new context, free of the discourse of blame and shame that often has otherwise stained their consciousness and influenced their personal development.

Whatever one's family background, there are stories to dig out that are pure gold. A youngster's grandmother might have been a nurse in Jamaica or Tobago. Or their grandfather might have been a fireman in Detroit who risked his life to save a small child. A great-great grandmother may have escaped slavery and earned enough money to free her children as well. Any fragment of a story can be part of a adolescent's life-giving narrative.

After years of experience in Yemin Orde we have become convinced that it is indeed possible to reveal in every teenager the hidden desire to find that their ancestors' lives contain a very special hidden quality that represents the secret source of their own strength.

Narratives to Live by

The teenage years are nourished by all kind of narratives. Doesn't this suggest a deep need for stories that are connected to their own lives? Teenagers read books, see movies, watch television, and listen to popular songs on the radio – devouring hundreds of stories in the process. The exposure of teenagers to this deluge of narratives suggests that it is worth our while to tell our family stories with a consciousness and artfulness that will allow them to stand up on their own, and not only be stored in adolescent minds as a collection of random snippets of information that they may have heard in passing. Our intent should be that family stories be absorbed into the bloodstream of youngsters and become part of their bone marrow.

If the framework a teenager is living in has its own narrative, stories that tell them "This is what we are like," a balance and equilibrium is created. In the face of the manufactured narratives he or she encounters on the screen, a teenager who knows their family's stories can say, "I, too, am part of a story." He or she becomes less susceptible to the lure of the empty, exchangeable stories offered on the TV screen, which like junk food, are outwardly appealing, but cannot ultimately satisfy the hunger for identity. Ideally, a family should have a continuously growing repertoire of stories about parents, grandparents, uncles and family friends. Every family has stories that illustrate faith or diligence, success against all odds, escape from danger, and also the varieties of human weaknesses. Jokes and funny incidents should also become part of the family "canon."

Rejection a Form of Success

The creation and extension of family myth should continue despite the apparent disinterest of adolescents, or their hostility. Teenagers may say, "Enough already, I don't want to hear about the day Grandpa saved that girl's life." It is not necessary to force stories down teenage throats, but we should never let their seeming rejection deter our efforts either. We have spent decades training ourselves in our Village to understand and to accept that adolescents' rejection of various messages is a kind of success in itself. We have had to internalize the notion that rejection in most of its forms is indeed part and parcel of the identity formation process. Like dough being kneaded, in which what was one minute on the surface is the next deep inside, all in preparation for rising, so, too, is teenage acceptance and rejection of our messages, stories, and values. Family myth is a potent vitamin in teenagers' nutrition, despite their displays of indifference or antagonism. When teenagers feel they are part of an ongoing story – whose upcoming chapters they will have a hand in creating – the existential loneliness in which they often live is sweetened and diminished.

The mythmaking quality of stories, however, should not be exaggerated. Stories should not be a closed circle, but should stimulate discussion and debate. Even old family stories should be the occasion, sometimes, for analysis. "Did Uncle Paul really do the right thing when he turned in that criminal to the police?" The ongoing challenges that each family faces should be woven into stories that through argument and dialogue reach upwards, inwards and outwards.

Chapter Seventeen

Reverence for the Past

Erasmus is Beating Up Kant

The very physical environment in our village aims to instill a reverence for the past and a feeling of its continued presence in our lives. In one's wildest dreams who could imagine the Catholic reformist philosopher, Erasmus of Rotterdam, encountering the staid German philosophical rationalist, Immanuel Kant, in a fist fight? Yet this was exactly the report I received from a breathless young messenger one unforgettable night, "Erasmus is beating up Kant."

What he meant to say in his telegraphic manner was that youngsters from the children's home named after Erasmus were engaged in a row with youngsters from the Kant house. Names like Aristotle, Marcus Aurelius, Sallah A Din, Maimonides, Deborah the Prophet and David Ben Gurion live with the children in their day-to-day life.

Teenagers have the capacity to see themselves as part of something larger and greater, and not only through identification with their ancestors. Their culture and ethnic group, and even the recent history that shaped the reality in which they live, can also be a source of strength and can cushion and heal the fear of their emergence into a fragmented world.

I have often noticed how Ethiopian immigrant children seem less traumatized by divorce than do children from Western families. I believe that this is because Ethiopian culture emphasizes the extended family. Children grow up knowing hundreds of family members going back several generations. The extended family allows broad possibilities for identification and modeling. Surrounded by uncles, aunts and cousins, divorce is far less threatening because it does not touch the extended family, which remains intact as the primary context of family life and a crucible of identity.

Origins are Food for the Future

A strong sense of identification with one's origins can serve a similar purpose. It can give a child the sense of being held in a much broader embrace, which is steadier and longer lasting than one's individual family and its circumstances. I recall two young teenagers who came to the village after their father murdered their mother – a more terrible or total negation of family can hardly be imagined. These two boys were children of Tunisian immigrants, and I worked hard to reinforce the pride in ethnic origins that was already nascent within them. They graduated Yemin Orde with a strong sense of identification with the Tunisian community that compensated, at least partly, for the destruction of their family. Instead of feeling an utter sense of alienation from their past they connected to a collective past, placing their private wounds into a broader arena that allowed healing to happen.

Over the years, a continuous involvement in the collective past of all the different groups of adolescents in the Village has become a fundamental part of the Yemin Orde method. There is often a great poignancy to these efforts, because by creating identification and pride and reinforcing the youngsters' sense of the continuous sweep of time, one is often also touching places of wounds and pain.

For example, the Ethiopian immigrants often arrive in Yemin Orde with feelings of cultural inferiority. Ethiopian immigrants come from a technologically undeveloped society into a country where high-tech is associated with high prestige. In Ethiopian villages, cooperative living was the norm; in Israel, the economy currently emphasizes competition, not cooperation. Some of the negative feelings Ethiopian children might have about their culture of origin are based on their own comparisons and inner conclusions. Their parents seem powerless and penniless compared to other Israelis. Israeli society is child-oriented, and immigrant children pick this up by watching television shows or observing their classmates in school and their relationship to their parents.

In contrast, Ethiopian culture places great emphasis on the status of elders and on responsibility to the community. Almost every weekend, children leave their beds and sleep on the floor of the living room in order to accommodate the numerous members of the extended family who often come for visits. But even beyond the children's own resentments and observations, children absorb messages from the society at large. Uneducated Israelis, and even much of the elite, often look at the Ethiopians as coming from "the jungle," from a primitive society less competent, and thus less valuable, than that of the West.

The message we bring these children is that far from being inferior, their culture is, in some important ways, superior to that of the West. We try to show them that the values that guided Ethiopian society contain abundant human wisdom. That the Ethiopian village elders were sophisticated students of human nature from whom our own judges and politicians would be wise to learn. That Ethiopia has a history as long and as varied as that of Europe. Since some sectors in Israeli society, chiefly those ultra-Orthodox who are of Eastern European background, have questioned the Jewishness of Ethiopian immigrants, we bring Ethiopian teenagers an unequivocal message that Ethiopian Jews were one of the most faithful and devout

Jewish communities anywhere. We try to imbed these messages in the daily life of our Village. The Village in its entirety celebrates the *Sigid*, a holiday unique to Ethiopian Jews. The eternal lamp that decorates the Village synagogue, at its very center, is named for some of the prominent Ethiopian Jewish spiritual leaders. When I first traveled to Ethiopia prior to Operation Solomon, several children each day were dying of disease in the urban slums where the Jewish community lived as they waited to immigrate to Israel. There I met a wise and gentle Ethiopian Jewish elder, Zowdu Zegaye, who was then invited to live full time at the Village, when the second massive wave of Ethiopian children came pouring into Yemin Orde. Now nearing seventy, he serves as a living fount of Ethiopian heritage for the children to absorb.

Most of the Ethiopian teenagers are familiar with the parables that adults from Ethiopia traditionally tell their children. We retell these stories, and then discuss their meaning, so that instead of remaining a childhood memory, these parables can become an integral part of their psyche as they reach new stages of intellectual development. They discover, in the process, that the stories their parents told them are far more sophisticated than they once thought.

Yemin Orde makes similar efforts for the children from other cultures as well. That is why every year the entire Village celebrates the 9th of May, the date on which Hitler's forces surrendered to the Soviet army. Not that there is a lack of Jewish and Israeli holidays. Moreover, no one in mainstream Israeli society celebrates May 9th. But on our mountaintop it is a major holiday. The suffering of the Russian people fighting against evil during World War II is a subject that transcends the failures of Communist society, and can be celebrated equally by Jewish and non-Jewish Russians.

We try to keep alive the memory of Alexander

Sergeyvish Pushkin, the great poet, whose birthday we joyously celebrate. And so, in our talks, we inculcate appreciation of great Russian literary heroes, artists and composers whom the teens would have heard about at home, but whose accomplishments find little expression in Israeli society. The Russian origin of most of Israel's early pioneers is also emphasized.

We also encourage our teens to keep improving their language of origin. Nothing can replace the deep emotional associations of the language you spoke as a child. Continuing to develop the ability to express oneself in this language gives important access to childhood feelings, and increases the possibility of interpreting them. Thus, our Village school offers courses in all the native languages of our students, including Amharic, Russian and Portuguese. We serve special dinners of Russian, Oriental, Brazilian and Ethiopian food, accompanied by stories, photos, and films that give a sense of the history and life of the place in question. The message is clear: *Origins are food for nourishing the future.*

Chapter Eighteen
Anchors in the Future

Lungs and Legs for the Marathon of Life

The future should be very much on our minds as we reinforce in our adolescent a sense of the past, of where they have been as individuals, as part of a family or a culture. Because, when we animate the past, give it vitality for our teenagers within their existential present, we are creating within them a dimension where subjective time can live. Connecting them to widening dimensions of personal and collective history, we deepen their ability to forge an identity that is not lost in the exigencies of the present, but rather anchored in the past and the future, in long-term plans and processes. What we really want our children to feel is that they are most alive through the satisfaction of the continuities they form. We want them to be psychologically fit for the long haul.

When we help our children develop an appreciation for how the past flows into the future like a living stream, we are giving them lungs and legs for running the marathon of life. For along with the courage to experiment and change, our children will need staying power, the ability to make and keep long-term commitments. In love, in professional life, in making a contribution to humanity, the race is not won by the swift, but by those whose stamina is fed by the long view of life, by those for whom the past and future, and not only the present, are real.

The goal is for our children to be able to see themselves as an extension of the collective. We are not talking only about legitimizing ethnicity or about creating pride in the minority culture of a teenager's family. Children from the most mainstream of families need to be able to feel connected to their history, to the sweep of time, to locate the thread from which the story of their life begins within the tapestry of history's narrative. Thus, it is not enough to merely teach history.

Teenagers need to hear that they are part of a history. They need to hear tales of heroism, enterprise or self-sacrifice and to be told that the stories indicate something about their own potential. They need to hear about traditions of wisdom, justice and creativity, and understand that as heirs to these traditions, they are the ones who will carry these traditions into the future.

This takes focused intention by parents and educators. One must mentally see the way the time-line anchored in the past points right through a teenager's existential present and into the future.

Emotionally as well as intellectually, adolescents need an anchor in the future in order to be able to explore the present, as well as to explore themselves and to experiment with their own identity. The crux of identity is the knowledge that you remain somehow the same through all the transformations and upheavals that the world bestows. Acquiring a stable identity means being able to project your notion of self, your ego, your "I" into the future as well as unifying the fragmented aspects of the past. If I have an anchor in the past and in the future, my "I" will be able to experience the present. But if I have no anchor in the future, I will not be able to be present in the here and now. To the extent that I feel the flow of time as a broad stream passing through me, each moment, each fragment of the present will be crowned for me with an aura of wholeness.

Vittorio

Few have a story as dramatic as that of Vittorio, who came

to our Village from Milano, Italy. Vittorio's parents divorced when he was six years old and his mother tried to rebuild her life with a series of men. When Vittorio was 10, his father moved to Israel. Around the same time, his mother became involved with a local man who moved into their household and eventually took Vittorio and his mother to live in a small town in the Tuscany region, several hours drive from Florence. Vittorio's mother gave birth to a baby boy, a little brother who came to mean a great deal to Vittorio.

Vittorio had been raised as a traditional Jew and his new stepfather, who was a lapsed Catholic, had in the first flush of romance expressed interest in learning about Judaism and even converting. But when the family moved out of Milan, Vittorio's stepfather returned to Catholicism, and forbade his wife to keep a kosher kitchen. Vittorio stubbornly refused to give up on his family's religious traditions, which stretched back for centuries. Every week, he would take a lengthy train ride to Milan, where his paternal grandmother lived. She would cook for him, and provide him with meat for the coming week that she had bought at the kosher butcher.

Vittorio finished elementary and junior high school and began to think about high school. His stepfather tried to convince him that he had better forget about pursuing any career that required academic skill or even perseverance.

"You're a nothing, you're a nobody," he would tell him. "You don't have the strength or the concentration to study."

Vittorio's stepfather registered him for a high school that taught watch repair, telling him "That's the best you can hope for."

Vittorio was confused. Although his confidence had been damaged by his parents' divorce and his stepfather's hurtful words, he still did not fully accept that his future horizons were as limited as his stepfather portrayed them. The summer before high school Vittorio decided to visit his father in Israel, as if to discover another part of himself.

His stepfather was livid. "If you go," he said, "Don't bother coming back."

"Fine," Vittorio answered. "I won't come back."

When Vittorio arrived in Israel, he faced more disappointment. From what he knew his father was still single and living alone. But when he knocked on the door of his father's flat in Ashkelon, a city in the south of Israel, he discovered that his father had remarried and had a new infant son. It quickly became apparent that his father and new stepmother did not intend to invite him to live with them.

"The apartment is too small," his father said. But what he really meant was that his new life had no space in it for a teenage son. Vittorio's father offered him a choice of two boarding situations in which he could attend school. Both were located several hours away from Ashkelon – a clear hint at the distance from his life that Vittorio's father wished to keep him. One of them, the one Vittorio chose, was Yemin Orde Youth Village.

When Vittorio arrived in our Village, he was withdrawn and surrounded by a cloak of sadness. But within a year, he began to be recognized for the sensitive, intelligent and highly competent person he already showed signs of becoming. In my conversations with him I learned his story, and realized that the open wound of his mother's silent rejection, when his stepfather told him not to come back, she had said nothing, and he had not a single letter from her the entire first year he was in the village, needed to be addressed. I encouraged Vittorio to keep writing letters to his mother.

"This way, you know that you have acted like a son

should," I told him. "One day you will be able to say to her," I promised, "You abandoned me, but I never abandoned you."

My subliminal message to Vittorio, which I repeated in various ways over and over again, was: *You are stronger than your mother. You are not destined to hurt and disappoint those who love you as she has.* I also tried to instill in him the notion that he could draw energies of survival from earlier generations: *The degradations of your parents' generation need not reflect on you. Go back further, to your grandparents and beyond. Life takes place along a long axis, it is the expression and realization of all the previous generations – your parents, not you, are the aberration, the weak link in the chain of love and loyalty that has forged your family.*

These messages provided Vittorio with foundations anchored in the past and the future upon which he could rebuild his shattered inner world. On the one hand, he had an image of a concrete promise for the future, the day when, strong and confident, he would approach his mother and tell her, "I never abandoned you." On the other hand, he was encouraged in his ability to draw strength from his family's past, as reflected in his grandmother's personality and devotion to him.

By creating anchors for him in the past and the future we were able to liberate his present, at least relatively, from the threatening grip of his past disappointments and his anxiety about the future. Within this island of consciousness, he had space in which to function in day-to-day life and to absorb new knowledge and insights, and to slowly regain his self-confidence.

Vittorio was extremely attentive to the messages that I take care to plant in my open discussions with all the youngsters. He recalls that he identified so strongly with one of the sayings that was repeated in those discussions that it became a kind of mantra for him.

"The fox will speak in its own time," says Rashi, the 12th century Jewish sage, meaning, "Be patient. Falsehood eventually fades and the truth will have its day."

This sense of destiny and ultimate justice, reinforced by his daily life in the Village, helped him internalize the faith that nothing had to be rushed, because that day of reckoning would indeed come.

And it did, sooner than might have been expected. At the end of two years we supported Vittorio's desire to sample the fruits of future promise by returning to Italy during the summer to visit his mother. With Yemin Orde's help, Vittorio got a summer job washing dishes at a kibbutz. After six weeks, he had managed to save up for a trip to Italy. The rabbi of Florence, who knew Vittorio and his story, offered to drive him up to the village where his mother and her new husband lived. No sooner had they parked in front of Vittorio's mother's home than his stepfather appeared, fierce and grim.

"We don't want this boy here," the stepfather said, speaking to the rabbi as if Vittorio did not exist.

"It's alright, I just came to say hello," Vittorio said, ignoring the slight.

"Your mother does not want to see you," the stepfather replied. The rabbi started the car and began to drive away, but before they had traveled more than a few meters Vittorio saw, through the second story window, a shadowy figure – his little brother. His heart leaped, and he asked the rabbi to stop the car. With a great shout, he addressed his mother, who he still had not seen. "Goodbye, Mama. This is it. You are never going to see me again." Within a few seconds his mother had raced down the stairs and embraced him.

Their conversation lasted only a few minutes, but Vittorio felt that he had won a great victory, as though he had succeeded in planting a flag on the territory of his childhood despite all the attempts to evict him. The effort to allow Vittorio to experience a taste of the perfected future, even before the end of his adolescence, became another turning point in his road to a successful adulthood.

We have seen this process many times with adolescents who were separated from their childhood homes. If we manage to help them return to the place they left, whether in Eastern Europe, Ethiopia or elsewhere, equipped with new self-confidence and perspective, they often achieve a sense of inner unity, thereby healing wounds that previously left open. It is important to know that we don't have to wait until adulthood and its various therapeutic modalities to close up the open wounds caused by abandonment. It may not be an exaggeration to compare this process to medical interventions that cure potential defects in embryos before they are born into the light of the world. Adolescents can seal wounds and close circles while still in their teenage years, thus sparing them years of suffering and search in adulthood.

Nir

From my childhood I have had a special craving for chocolate mousse. During the early years of the State of Israel, chocolate mousse was a delicacy available only once a year, on Independence Day. But the best chocolate mousse I ever tasted was only recently, in a small restaurant in south Tel Aviv. The mousse was good, but the taste was sweeter because of the circumstances. The restaurant's owner, Nir, was once a child from a home in which the parents mostly fought with each other. When life at home became unbearable, Nir was placed at Yemin Orde.

Of the many children who have been able to emerge out of their childhood chaos, and have actually transformed the materials of their tragic childhood experiences into a life-giving response, Nir's story is almost too perfect an example of poetic justice. Nir hovered over me as I ate, asking me how my mousse tasted every few spoonfuls. Behind him, I could see his father diligently working the cash register and his mother occasionally peeking out from behind a ledge and bringing trays of food out from the kitchen where she was cooking.

"How are they getting along these days?" I asked Nir.

"They had better get along," he told me, only half joking. "I told them the first day of work that the moment they begin to fight, they're both fired."

I knew he meant it, and by the fact that the work went smoothly, I also knew that they had adjusted accordingly.

I was deeply impressed by Nir's ability to articulate and analyze what had made his parents so violent before and why they were now able to be part of a working team. A crucial part of Nir's rehabilitation at Yemin Orde were our efforts to instill in him an anticipatory scheme – an inner awareness of his future possibilities – that his home environment was not able to provide. For all our children who have emerged from an emotionally fragmented childhood, the ability to internalize that the era of fragmentation is over and that the flow of time is indeed leading to a better place has been continually reinforced by convincing living examples. By exposing the children presently in our care to a constant tide of graduates who had moved beyond their traumatic early years into vibrant young adulthood, we instill in them a clear sense of direction and positive expectations.

Nir, after gaining control of his life, went one step further. He implanted within the fulfilled future a mended form of his broken past, a belated fulfillment of a child's dream. As a child he was powerless in the face of the bitter arguments that poisoned the atmosphere in his home. Now, with the economic power in his hands, he used it to insure that his parents would have to work together in harmony.

Including the Future in the Present

To what extent should children and adolescents be encouraged to anticipate adulthood? Medieval paintings often portray children as tiny adults, with sharp, thin faces seemingly already carved and defined by life's travails. In renaissance paintings children recover their special beauty, innocence and baby fat. But the nature and meaning of childhood and its relationship to adult life continue to be shaped by historical circumstances and debated by scholars.

Are adolescence and childhood time periods whose value and meaning are inherent? Or should these stages be understood and appreciated mainly as a time of preparation for adulthood? This is a question that psychologists and educational philosophers have grappled with at length during the last half century, and, at least in the realm of theory, the child-centered school of thought has emerged victorious. And rightfully so. The "discovery" that childhood is a time that deserves to be treated and considered on its own is one of the great insights of the past generation. For the child-centered educator, childhood and adolescence cease to be seen primarily as an opportunity to shape and influence young lives in order to ready them for the future. This allows parents and educators to let children live in the present, and gives legitimacy to children's own natural paths to self-expression, thus freeing them from the expectation that they be miniature adults.

And yet, especially where adolescents are concerned, the future, like the past, cannot be ignored. Although there has been a great deal of emphasis recently on educating children and teens to be able to function in new and unknown situations, this approach is valid only up to a point. A future that remains entirely unknown, no matter how much training in improvisation is given, will be a source of anxiety for a teenager. The future must also be touched upon, represented, and thus included within the teenager's existential present. If the past and future are not somehow present in the adolescent's here and now, unresolved wounds inflicted by past traumas and the menacing threat looming from an unknown future will shadow their consciousness.

As already pointed out, time is the primary substance from which the mind shapes its identity. The flow of time emerges from both the personal and collective past and courses towards the future. As much as our psyche is shaped by our experiences in the past, our minds are also structured to anticipate the future. If we perceive the future as threatening and chaotic, we will be too filled with anxiety to live fully in the present.

This is especially true in adolescence. For while children have some capacity to retreat into worlds of their own even when surrounded by evil and cruelty, like the boy in Begnini's film, *Life is Beautiful*, adolescents generally do not have that ability. The remarkable life force that powers their physical, sexual and intellectual spurt towards adulthood is programmed to turn them outwards, towards the real world. When their image of the future in the real world is beyond their grasp, when they have no ability to picture themselves in coming stages of life, teens may attempt to withdraw into a dream world, with disastrous affects. We can imagine the various stages of life as a series of consecutive platforms.

But what if the next platform is drifting away beyond our ability to reach it? What if the future is colored not with promise, but rather vague and undifferentiated threat, tinted by the projection of negative past experiences?

Suspended Animation

And without question, the future does loom threateningly. By the time children reach adolescence, they will have seen thousands of images of apocalyptic violence from the television, movies and comics. They will have absorbed hundreds of sound bites or texts predicting economic, environmental or political disaster. They will have tuned in to their parents' anxieties about the future, which has become more complex and less predictable than at other times in human history.

Children and adolescents have a built-in relationship with the future that determines much of their present mode of being and nourishes the contents of their self. Healthy growing up is marked by an increasing ability to infuse rational thought into one's relationship with the future. The "moratorium" from work and responsibility that was created after the spread of industry and the rise of urban centers was conceived as a time that would be devoted to preparing youngsters for their role in a newly complex society. Yet what of the emotional vulnerability of young people existing in a state of suspended animation, bereft of the status and identity that responsibility and a stable family life give?

The teenage years are considered a period during which crucial skills are acquired. Yet, they are also emotionally formative. They can be formative in a negative sense if the teenager's relationship with the future becomes so saturated with fear that the idea of the future becomes overwhelmingly burdensome. The teenage years need to be a moratorium, yet one in which self-confidence can grow. It has always been my axiomatic belief that adults have a major role to play in liberating adolescents from the dark, threatening mist that hovers on the horizon for many teens.

The Bouncing Affect

Moreover, the adolescent concept of the future is vulnerable to what we call "the bouncing affect." Since children's basic feelings about reality are formulated through the prism of their own experience, it is natural for them to "bounce" their experience of the past onto their expectations for the future. A child that has experienced abandonment in the past will most likely fear abandonment in the future. Expectations for the future, which often means fears about the future, are bounced back into the present, in the form of free-floating anxiety, and children stuck between a fragmented past and an unpredictable future will not abandon themselves to the present.

In contrast, adolescents in whom seeds of faith in the future have been implanted will be better able to throw themselves into the present. This can be seen clearly in intellectual pursuits. Fear and anxiety are one of the most significant obstacles to intellectual achievement, especially in fields that demand problem-solving abilities and the capacity to explore the unknown. Children who lack faith in the future are like Noah's dove before the earth was dry enough to provide her with a perch. She had to keep circling back to the ark – to the same situation, the same patterns of thought.

The poet John Keats, once remarked that part of Shakespeare's greatness was in his "negative capability," his capacity to enter the unknown in his poems and plays without attempting to determine or define their outcome from the start. Shakespeare's characters often meet tragic ends, because they lack the very quality of which their creator was so well possessed. Shakespeare's two most famous adolescent characters, Romeo and Juliet, are prime examples. Out of fear that they will be separated they rush to marry, and in doing so neglect to adequately strategize and communicate, or even to fully perceive reality. Romeo, of course, believes Juliet to be dead, when she is in fact still alive, and commits suicide himself.

We want our teenagers to develop the "negative capability" that Romeo and Juliet lacked – the ability to be relaxed in the face of what is unknown, and patient before the dark rush of time. Thus many of our arguments with our teenagers have to do with the urgencies they feel, their need to do something "Now!" Unfortunately, we often respond with urgencies of our own, instead of demonstrating the patience we want them to learn.

Chapter Nineteen
Seeds of Faith in the Future

Bedrock Messages

How can we implant in children seeds of faith in the future? How do we create this anchor? Parenthood and the essentially parental quality of good educators means being able to send an unequivocal message to our teens that any kind of abandonment is not a possibility for them, as far as we are concerned. The fear of abandonment, amplified for many teenagers because of their experiences in their early life and the 'unfinished business' of their childhood, is perhaps the primary source of anxiety about the future. We have to instill in our young ones an absolute, unmistakable sense of our commitment to them for as long as we live.

In our Village the primary way we reassure adolescents about the future is not through words. Teenagers know, both instinctively and through bitter experience, that talk is cheap and promises are made to be broken. On the other hand, concrete lessons are worth a thousand words. We therefore have built a Graduates House, with space for dozens of graduates, a place in the Village that our youngsters pass several times a day. Every adolescent at Yemin Orde knows that we consider being part of our community a lifetime commitment, that we never have and never will abandon graduates. They will always be welcome in the Village and at the Graduates House.

There are always graduates returning to Yemin Orde, both at high and low points in their life. Life in Yemin Orde is punctuated by the wedding celebrations that we host for graduates, as well as celebrations of their achievements in the National Service and in the academic world. Graduates regularly return to Yemin Orde to teach workshops or organize exhibitions, and give back to the community some of what they have received. Every weekend, graduates join children's tables in the dining hall to tell about their experiences in the outside world and answer questions. Perhaps the greatest gift they bestow is the gift of their presence, which reminds the teens now living here that their relationship with Yemin Orde will continue into the indefinite future.

It is not only the graduates who have succeeded, however, who are welcome in Yemin Orde. The Graduates House is also meant to serve as a sort of refuge for those graduates who are in a period of crisis. This, too, is important for the teenagers who are living here to see.

Recently, one of our graduates, Eitan, who had escaped destructive parents and flourished during the latter part of adolescence, was unfortunate enough to experience their toxic influence in his life again. He began a drug and drinking binge that ended in a police lockup in the southern city of Eilat. Yemin Orde sent another of its graduates, one of the first Ethiopian immigrants to study law in Israel, to convince the judge to release Eitan to our custody. Eitan came "home" to Yemin Orde, where he continued to cause havoc, wrecking the room we gave him.

Seeing graduates who have returned to Yemin Orde at a time of crisis tells the teens still in our Village that our promise to remain in our graduates' lives is unconditional. After Eitan's destructive weekend in Yemin Orde, several youngsters approached me and said, "Now we really understand what you mean when you say you will always be with us."

There are those who criticize the Yemin Orde method by saying that it fosters dependency. Yet in my experience, only about 10% of Yemin Orde graduates ever need our continued help after finishing high school. Most have gained the self confidence to make it on their own, and their continued involvement with the Village is part of their way to give back some of what they have been given. Of graduates who do need our help, only a very small percentage – perhaps one in a hundred – develops what might be termed dependency. Once in a decade, a graduate develops what might be termed *hostile* dependency, something that is hard to bear and is akin to the bad relationships that sometimes develop within families. This is a price we are willing to pay to plant the seeds of confidence in the future in hundreds of other youngsters in our community every year. And even this small group has its purpose. Like Eitan, they show the current group of youngsters that Yemin Orde really conforms to the poet Robert Frost's definition of home: "The place where, when you have to go there, they have to let you in."

'We Will Never Leave You'

Parents, too, should internalize the notion that it is incumbent on them to provide their teenager with a sense of confidence about the future. When our own inner insecurities make this seem impossible, we would do well to remember that for our children we are a representation of the direction in which their future may be heading. This thought may be just what we need in order to catalyze our efforts to keep ourselves together. A pathetic representation of adulthood is for our children like a disturbing prophecy about their own future. Sometimes, when we desperately seek answers to explain our children's undesirable behaviors, it might be valuable to reassess the kind of adult posture that we display for them. I do not mean to suggest that parents need to sacrifice emotional authenticity in order to appear as a determined pillar of strength. However,

I do suggest that parents recognize their own inner value and the sense of achievement and fulfillment that is available to them through the task of parenting. This does not exclude consciously exposing children to our weaknesses and pain. But the awareness of what we mean to our children, both as parents and as a representative of humanity, should provide us with a transforming charge of significance and weight at least when we are in our role as parents.

In looking at our adolescents it may seem to us as if they are completely absorbed in the moment, and that the future is the last thing on their mind. I have learned over the years, again and again, that in the structure of the adolescent psyche the future is already inescapably present and of real and deep concern. Most adolescents are incapable of or reluctant to express this; in fact there may be an inverse relationship between the willingness of a teenager to talk about the future and the extent to which this concern occupies him or her. Those adolescents who are obsessed with thoughts about their future may be the last ones to share such thoughts. Teenagers may treat their fears and dreams of the future as a sort of pregnancy, where the embryo remains hidden and protected inside its mother's body until it can survive the light of day. Even those children who don't seem to want us to take an active role in helping them imagine the future need us to provide positive reinforcement for their hidden agenda.

In providing basic confidence about the future our Village has to make an extra effort to express what is taken for granted within a stable parental home. Parents are parents for a lifetime, no matter what either they or their children do. Adolescents know, at least in the great majority of cases, that the door to their childhood home will still be open for them during the years of their young adulthood and perhaps even beyond. They know that there is a drawer or a corner in the attic where their report cards and drawings from first grade are being stored for posterity (although it probably wouldn't hurt to take one of those drawings, frame it and put it up in the living room.) They know that their parents will be the grandparents to their children, though again, dreaming out loud from time to time about one day holding your son or daughter's baby in your arms might be a good way of strengthening your teen's anchor in the future. Even though these glimpses of the future may seem farfetched in the present, we have learned over the course of years that they are seeds that can eventually grow into prophecies fulfilled.

Although the parent-child relationship is meant to last for life, many parents empower the threatening aspect of the future in a conscious or unconscious way. Too often they believe that they are doing so for the child's own good. Parents tend to warn children they consider lazy or spendthrift that "At 18, you are on your own. That's what my father did to me." Thus threat becomes an intergenerational myth, penetrating even deeper into the psyche. Or parents may talk about the impending years of their own old age and infirmity, in order to give the same message of "I won't always be able to take care of you."

I always advise against this type of warning. Whatever might be gained in terms of inspiring independent behavior in the short run – and it is not at all certain that there would be such gains – the down side of such messages in the long-term, in terms of confidence lost, is too great. On the contrary, it is in the interest of the adolescent that the parents convey a sense of their continuing presence in the future no matter what.

I am reminded in this context of a famous story about Rabbi Yisrael Baal Shem Tov, the founder of the Hasidic movement. Yisrael was born late in his father's life, and he was orphaned at the age of five. As his father lay dying, he called little Yisrael to his side, clasped his hand, and said to him, "Never be afraid, for I promise you that God will always be with you."

Later in life, Rabbi Yisrael Baal Shem Tov testified that this promise was a major source of strength for him. The point here is that Yisrael's father knew that he would not be able to be a physical presence in his son's life, but that he could, through his promise, be a spiritual presence by being the source of his faith in God's continuing protection and guidance. In the same way we are not lying when we convey to our adolescents the message that we will be with them in the future as we are with them now. By becoming a source of confidence for our children at this critical point in their lives, we really do accompany them into the future, living within them as a continuing source of strength.

Arousing Fear of Abandonment

There are other, subtler ways in which parents often unwittingly intensify their children's fear of the future. Many of us express anger through coldness, withdrawal and even by verbalizing threats of severing the relationship. We may threaten expulsion from the home – "I'll send you to military school" – or express another kind of limited or extensive excommunication. During these flash points of anger, at least from the teenage perspective, the relationship between parents and children is revealed to be contingent and conditional. There is some legitimacy to this perspective. The Talmud says that people reveal their true personality in three different ways: when called upon to be generous with their money, when drunk and when angry. Anger that expresses itself as emotional distancing can easily arouse teenagers' fears of abandonment, which they may have successfully suppressed since early childhood.

Another way that parents sometimes enhance the

sense of threat emanating from the future is by expressing too specific a dream about their children's future accomplishments. The borderline between encouraging your children to believe in themselves and turning them into the proxy fulfillment of your own fantasies is sometimes dangerously thin. Parents would do well not to dwell on the college or profession that they think suits their children, but instead give them the sense that they have many options, all of which, depending on their own predilections and needs, are acceptable. By locking in on one possibility – that your daughter be a physician, or your son a violinist – you risk evoking anxiety over the possibility that they will be unable to fulfill your fantasies. And even if they do become what you wish for them, they may not "own" their choices as fully as if they had come to them independently.

Similarly, it would be wise for parents not to dwell on the failures or setbacks of the children of friends who may be a few years older than their own children. The message must be that emotional acceptance is unconnected to performance. Children deserve to be loved by their parents even during moments of crisis or setback. On the other hand, with adolescents who may feel locked into their parents' fate, it is necessary to bolster their faith that it is possible to break free of what they see as a cursed and closed intergenerational circuit. With them, suggesting possible directions backed by successful models may provide the desired breakthrough.

As parents we may think it is our duty to "drive" our children to success. It is important to remember that children who are driven can often end up feeling like they are being driven over a cliff; for example, that failure in academic or professional life is equivalent to death. If we are content with our career, our marriage or our social life, this will be transmitted to our children and have a long-lasting influence on them. It never hurts to also assess our inner world in reference to our children. What components of our lives are we not really happy about? There is a good chance that our adolescents, with their sensitive antennae, will have traced these places a long time ago. We might as well attune our own antennae to the same channel. To the extent that we become conscious of where we feel we have failed, we will be less likely to transmit this feeling to our children as something inevitable. As a result, frustrations will be reduced and expectations more realistic.

Chapter Twenty
Keeping the Flame Alive

Quest for Justice

While some of the qualities that characterize adolescence need to follow their natural course and disappear before maturity can be reached, the intrinsic quest for justice is not one of these. There are people whose psyche remains pathologically stuck in adolescence, and this can cause much unhappiness. If the restless search for sexual identity or the fits of rebellious anger that characterize adolescence are still controlling influences in the life of a forty-year old, something has gone wrong. But the passion for justice, that inner vector that breaks outwards towards the world, is precious and should be shielded and nourished even while the adolescent's moral judgment continues to develop to new heights. This flame can be the fountainhead for the whole psyche. If we want it to keep burning, and not sputter out in young adulthood, we have to provide it with fuel during adolescence. Our experiences in adolescence largely determine whether our passion for justice and *Tikkun Olam* are forever extinguished or provided with the inspiration to last a lifetime.

Carrying the flame of justice into adulthood can ease the burden of unfinished business and emotional wounds by shifting us from our egocentricity and marking our individuality with transcendent significance. To the extent that the years following adolescence involve a struggle for personal success and survival, they can bend people and make them adjust to a crooked reality, thus causing them to abandon the dream of justice as unattainable. Fuel to stoke their passion for justice must be stored for young people during their formative years. This fuel is accumulated by involving teenagers in an existential discourse formed through exposing and engaging them in efforts to right wrongs and see that justice is done, and supporting their actions to make the world a better place. It is important that teens experience the taste of at least partial victory or success in these efforts. This taste provides proof that the attainment of justice does not go against all the odds; that the utopian dream of a just world can actually penetrate the vessels of everyday reality.

Utopian dream, you may ask? What about the destructive and anti-social behaviors that make a bitter mockery of justice, that are often so characteristic of adolescence? Let's go back, for instance, to the phenomenon of theft in our Village, when it happened, that youth who had less stole from those who had more. More than once, teenagers who confessed to stealing explained their misdeeds as no less than acts of justice – efforts simply to redistribute wealth.

However misguided their application, much of teenage anger is connected to their highly developed sense of justice – educators are perceived as unfairly favoring other students, or parents other siblings – and provocations are committed as vigilante acts of protest. These acts are usually accompanied by a feeling of helplessness. When the elements that should be part of the teenage world, a sense of the past and future, ideals and so forth, are absent, adolescents will apply their instinct for justice to the shrunken world in which they find themselves. The consequence, often, is that the family itself will become a devastated battlefield.

Battles as Educational Tool

Broader horizons towards which an adolescent can sally forth may not seem like a magical formula. Yet our experience with educational programs geared to engage teenagers in ethical issues and questions of moral judgment is that they diminish phenomenon such as theft. No longer are teens as prone to distorting moral logic until their egotistical ends justified the means. Just reading the newspaper together with your teens and inviting debate on ethical issues is a good start. Trying to change the world through "battles" or projects, big or small, is even better. They can take aim at interest groups, bureaucracies, an unjust system or simply indifference. The "battle" could be to force the city to make a wheelchair access for handicapped people to the restrooms in a public park, or it could mean getting a hammer and nails and building the ramp on your own.

Battles are excellent educational tools, because they are focused, involve positions that need to be examined, interpreted and articulated, and because they create a circle of togetherness that includes you and your teenager. Letter writing campaigns, demonstrations, lobbying elected officials, information gathering – any forum in which you can involve your adolescent in fighting for a cause that both of you consider just will have a powerful affect as an educational tool. So will feeding the hungry, visiting the sick or lonely, and reading to the blind – especially when such activities are accompanied by a discussion of why they are necessary and what society can do in order to better take care of those who are in need.

En Hod: *Fighting Death*

As you can probably tell by now, at Yemin Orde there is almost always some kind of "battle" going on, often pitting the Village against some outside force. In these campaigns, we may end up appearing before a judge. Sometimes our fights make it all the way to the Israel Supreme Court. One never knows what the educational outcome of such real life encounters will be. For example, we recently went through the final stage of a battle against an artist's colony called En Hod, which is our next-door neighbor.

En Hod decided to set aside some land on the hill directly below the Village for use as a community cemetery. My intuition was that this was bad for our Village. My reasoning was that the last thing our youngsters should have to see when they look just beyond the borders of our Village is death. No small percentage of the youth living in our Village are orphans or have been abandoned by one parent or another. For many, our Village is the first experience of stability that they have had in a lifetime of uncertainty. I worried that the sight of a cemetery just outside the fence delineating the Village would send a negative message: *death is what is waiting for you beyond the safe haven of Yemin Orde.* At the very least, I felt, Yemin Orde should have been consulted before En Hod made its final plans.

We learned as much as we could about how to fight what we considered the improper use of land. This in itself was a revelation for many of the kids; that they can use their sense of justice to shape their environment! That they are not simply passive bystanders who must accept the decisions made for them by inaccessible and impersonal authorities! That they have the right to make themselves heard! Eventually, the case went to court. Yemin Orde staff attended the court case along with a group of representatives of the children who offered testimony to the judge. One result of our legal battle was that everyone in our Village was suddenly touching the motif of death. What is usually a taboo subject, one that often fascinates and scares teenagers, became an open topic of conversation, and thus lost some of its power to frighten.

Eventually, we lost the case. But we managed to find lessons even in the loss. During a group dynamics session on the lawn, I heard one teen saying to another that it was actually a nice thing that people from En Hod wanted to be buried near where they had lived. It meant, in this young person's eyes, that death was a continuation of life, not an absolute disruption. So in the end, even battles that are lost can turn into a source of insights, as the debate surrounding them builds a teenager's confidence in their ability to understand and interact with the world around them.

Acts of Heroism

Involving teens in recognizing and rewarding acts of heroism in the fight against evil also helps to affirm and reinforce their innate sense of justice. This past fall, an Israeli Arab teenager, about the same age as our students, succeeded in foiling a Palestinian suicide bomber who was on his way to blow himself up along with as many people as he could.

By chance, the young Israeli Arab, who is from a town 40 miles or so from our Village, sat next to the suicide bomber as they waited for a bus in the Hadera-bound station. In order to make room for himself as he sat down, he picked up the bomber's knapsack. It felt suspiciously heavy. He had a sudden hunch that his fellow traveler might be about to commit mass murder. Calmly, he borrowed the suicide bomber's cell phone, claiming that he had to tell his father he would be late, walked a few feet away and called the police. When the police arrived to check the story, the bomb went off, killing the suicide bomber and the policeman and injuring the Israeli Arab teen as he attempted to run for refuge, but taking many fewer lives than if he had succeeded in embarking on the bus.

Helped by a generous donor, we turned this story into a lesson that our teens would remember by "raising a flag," to transform the incident into a potent symbol for justice and good. First, in an open discussion with our teenagers, we decided that the flowers sent by the Israeli President and the chocolates sent by the Prime Minister were not enough to show the appreciation that this young man's heroic act deserved. Our youngsters visited him in the hospital. At a ceremony in his hometown attended by Village residents, we presented him with a check that we hoped would help him pay for the rest of his education.

Later, he slept over in our Village and we "adopted" him as an honorary member of our community. The message folded into our gift to him had several layers. By paying special attention to this young man, we showed that we honor those who put ethics above ethnic loyalties, and that we value the signs of hope that tell us that Jews and Arabs can save each other as well as kill each other. We tried to demonstrate that acts of heroism are important both in and of themselves and because they inspire others. And we showed that, as a community, we are given the opportunity to magnify the power of goodness by lending it our attention and expressing our identification and gratitude.

We try to continue nourishing stories like this over an extended period of time. In this case, we will continue to follow this young man's recovery and progress, and will find more occasions to appreciate his ethical choice in placing the value of human life over all other considerations. The story of his act and of how it moved us will become part of the story of the Village, part of our tradition, and thus part of the story of each teenager living here.

Real Struggles Mend Hearts

It is possible to take advantage of many different kinds of situations in order to introduce teenagers to the process of fighting for what is right. Sometimes, you don't even necessarily need to be right in order to turn a conflict into a learning experience. In my early years in the Village it did not have a proper sewage system or the money to have such a system installed. The Israeli Society for the Protection of Nature sued us because sewage flowing from the Village was polluting a fresh water stream in the valley below. The court subpoena outlining the case against us was posted on the central billboard and immediately became the talk of the Village.

While some of the Village teenagers rallied to the banner we had raised, others could be heard taking a cynical stance. "So what if the Village is being sued? I could care less," or "Why doesn't the Village get one of our supporters to pay for the sewage pipes?"

Even these responses to the Village's distress counted, for they brought to the surface feelings of abandonment that teenagers most often kept hidden. When adolescents identify a real struggle – not a theoretical debate about issues or an educational simulation, but an actual conflict or threat – it subtly touches the area of their scars and allows their exposure to the light of day. By saying "I could care less," a teenager is joining the discussion on justice in a way that is beyond the discourse on good and evil. What the teenager really means by "I could care less" is "Look at me. Do you think I was given an equal opportunity in life?" or "Who will compensate me for the suffering I have lived through?"

"Unless and until I am compensated for my pain," these teenagers are saying, "I have no interest in your campaigns." They thus signal their withdrawal into their own shrunken niche.

These conflicts afford teenagers the opportunity to express feelings that might otherwise be buried deep inside. Within the context of a real conflict, when the stakes are real, authentic feelings lying dormant within the teenager are activated and the opportunity for mending of the heart is created. This is especially true when teenagers who initially expressed cynicism are eventually pulled into the conflict, and come to understand that it is possible for justice to have its day; to win, or at least to take part in a fair struggle. Even when kids stay on the sidelines and watch, it gives them a chance, in an indirect and semi-conscious way, to work on their own feelings of having been victimized. On several occasions since I have been at the Village, the atmosphere created during the communal pursuit of justice has allowed teenagers to open up and reveal their stories of victimization, including the sexual molestation that some experienced as children in institutional homes.

In the case of the spilled sewage, fighting back against our accusers became an exercise in value-laden education á la John Dewey. We studied the maps of the area, the geological makeup of the region, the legal claims against us, the rules of court procedure and our possible lines of legal defense. We went as a group to talk to the Society for the Protection of Nature, and learned that it was not us who they were after. They were really using their attack on us as a strategy that would force government authorities to take action in regulating sewage flow and preventing pollution. A threat – "The Village is being sued" – thus transformed into a much more complex situation.

When we eventually went to court, one of our teenagers, a young Ethiopian Jewish woman, asked for permission to speak.

"You see," she said to the judge, "Most of our money comes from donations for specific buildings or projects, which bear the name of the donor." Here she was fudging a little bit, as our buildings are named after inspirational heroes like Maimonides, Immanuel Kant and Martin Luther King, not after our donors.

"What rich person is going to donate money for a sewage pipe?" The judge and the courtroom erupted in laughter. In the end we were forced to pay a small fine. But the greater reward was that several of our young people were inspired by this and other battles, and through their exposure to the legal system during this case, to become lawyers. In fact, two of them became the first attorneys from the Ethiopian immigrant community.

Is our tendency as parents to protect our children from the battles in which the family is involved justified? On the whole, parents should not give children the feeling that the struggles the family is engaged in are mysterious and beyond the ability of children to understand. When we have trouble in our Village, such as financial difficulties, it is not only the bookkeeping staff who knows and feels involved. In general, we try to create an atmosphere of financial transparency in the Village. We want the children to feel the vulnerability of adults just as they feel our strength.

I think that this not a bad practice for families as well. Whether in disputes with the neighbors, employers, or other family members, parents should explain the parameters and stakes of the battle and should open a discussion about both the ethical implications of the conflict and the strategies that could be pursued. Don't children, at the end of the day, almost always know about these battles anyway? Parents should act as buffers, as shock absorbers, protecting children from the raw and ugly aspects of conflict. But they should not expect to be silencers or censors.

Involving our teenagers in the struggles that engage us brings them into the circle of real life, like they were before the industrial revolution. It also affords parents the opportunity to raise their own standards of conflict. Instead of acting out of hurt and anger, parents who consciously include teenagers in their battles will have to clarify their stance in ethical terms in order to explain them to their children, and to modify their positions if that is what is called for.

Let your desire to fuel your adolescent's sense of justice guide you in restoring the sharpness of your own moral sense. Here, too, involving children in battles means acting from a place of wholeness and responsibility – not from our woundeds, the place where we have been hurt and shattered. Even revealing our vulnerability to our children, if done with intention and awareness, can become part of this wholeness. By including our children in our struggles, we strengthen our covenant with them. Together we are part of the human search for justice. Together we can change the world.

Books and Authors

Samuel Hugo Bergman (1883-1975) was a Czech-born, German and Israeli Jewish philosopher and educator, who taught at the Hebrew University in Jerusalem, Israel. His books include *Faith and Reason: An Introduction to Modern Jewish Thought* (1961).

John Bowlby (1907-1990) was a British psychoanalytic theorist and a researcher into human emotional development. Among his important works is *Attachment and Loss* (1973).

Martin Buber (1878-1965) was a renowned Austrian Jewish philosopher, theologian, writer and educator. Among his many books are *I and Thou* (1923) and *Paths in Utopia* (1946).

John Dewey (1859-1852) was an American philosopher, psychologist and educational reformer, and is recognized as one of the founders of the philosophical school called Pragmatism. Among his important books are *Human Nature and Conduct* (1922) and *Freedom and Culture* (1939).

Jonathan Franzen (1959-) is an American fiction writer. His book *The Corrections* won a National Book Award in 2002.

Franz Kafka (1883-1924) is widely considered among the greatest German-language writers of the 20th century. His works, published posthumously, include *The Trial* (1925) and *The Castle* (1926).

George B. Leonard (1923-) is an American journalist, writer, and a leader of the human potential movement. Among his books are *The Decline of the American Male* (1958) and *Education and Ecstasy* (1968).

Margaret Mahler (1897-1985) was a Hungarian child psychologist and psychoanalyst who made important contributions to the theory of child development.

Ian McEwan (1948-) is a British novelist. His book *Amsterdam* won the Booker prize in 1998. His other works include *A Child in Time* (1987), *Atonement* (2001) and *Saturday* (2005).

A.S. Neill (1883-1973) was a Scottish educator and founder of the Summerhill School in 1924. His book *Summerhill: A Radical*

Approach to Child Rearing (1960) became an international best seller.

Neil Postman (1931-1973) was an American educator, media theorist and cultural critic. His books include *Teaching as a Subversive Activity* (1969), *Technopoly: The Surrender of Culture to Technology* (1992) and *The End of Education: Redefining the Value of School* (1995).

Gershom Scholem (1897-1982) was a German-born, Jewish philosopher and historian, and the founder of modern academic research into *Kabbala* and Jewish Mysticism. Among his books are *Major Trends in Jewish Mysticism* (1941) and *The Messianic Idea in Judaism* (1971).

Donald Winnicott (1896-1971) was an English pediatrician, psychoanalyst and one of the most influential psychological theorists of the 20th century.